Peer Coaching

Other ASCD books by Pam Robbins

How to Plan and Implement a Peer Coaching Program
by Pam Robbins

Learning from Lincoln: Leadership Practices for School Success
by Harvey Alvy and Pam Robbins

The New Principal's Fieldbook: Strategies for Success
by Pam Robbins and Harvey Alvy

Pam Robbins

Peer
Coaching

to Enrich Professional Practice, School Culture, and Student Learning

ASCD

Alexandria, Virginia USA

1703 N. Beauregard St. • Alexandria, VA 22311-1714 USA
Phone: 800-933-2723 or 703-578-9600 • Fax: 703-575-5400
Website: www.ascd.org • E-mail: member@ascd.org
Author guidelines: www.ascd.org/write

Judy Seltz, *Executive Director;* Stefani Roth, *Publisher;* Genny Ostertag, *Director, Content Acquisitions;* Julie Houtz, *Director, Book Editing & Production;* Darcie Russell, *Senior Associate Editor;* Georgia Park, *Senior Graphic Designer;* Mike Kalyan, *Manager, Production Services;* Valerie Younkin, *Production Designer*

PAPERBACK ISBN: 978-1-4166-2024-2   ASCD product #115014

PDF E-BOOK ISBN: 978-1-4166- 2026-6; see Books in Print for other formats.

Quantity discounts: 10–49, 10%; 50+, 15%; 1,000+, special discounts (e-mail programteam@ ascd.org or call 800-933-2723, ext. 5773, or 703-575-5773). For desk copies, go to www.ascd. org/deskcopy

ASCD Member Book No. F15-7. ASCD Member Books mail to Premium (P), Select (S), and Institutional Plus (I+) members on this schedule: Jan, PSI+; Feb, P; Apr, PSI+; May, P; Jul, PSI+; Aug, P; Sep, PSI+; Nov, PSI+; Dec, P. For current details on membership, see www.ascd.org/ membership.

Library of Congress Cataloging-in-Publication Data
Robbins, Pamela.
   Peer coaching to enrich professional practice, school culture, and student learning: Pam Robbins.
      pages cm
   Includes bibliographical references and index.
   ISBN 978-1-4166-2024-2 (pbk. : alk. paper) 1. Teaching teams—United States. 2. Group work in education—United States. 3. Peer review—United States. 4. Mentoring in education—United States. 5. Teachers—In-service training—United States. I. Title.
   LB1029.T4R64 2015
   371.14'8—dc23
                                                                    2015002054

23 22 21 20 19 18 17 16 15   1 2 3 4 5 6 7 8 9 10 11 12

Dedicated to

Muriel Robbins,
a retired educator, musician, and
school counselor, who taught me that to facilitate
thinking and understanding, it is more powerful
to communicate with questions than with
statements and with feeling rather than force.

David Robbins,
a retired teacher, principal, and central office
administrator, whose actions reflected his words,
"In the end, it is all about relationships."

My husband, J. Ray Cubbage,
whose humility, integrity, and grace
are unparalleled, and whose spirit is a constant
source of inspiration.

Peer Coaching

to Enrich Professional Practice, School Culture, and Student Learning

Acknowledgments

I would like to express deep appreciation to Kim Gray for her dedication, wisdom, and commitment to laboring long hours to prepare the manuscript; to Genny Ostertag, Director, Content Acquisitions at ASCD, for her sage advice and guidance from the acquisitions stage to production; to Kathleen Florio, editor, for the careful attention to detail during the editing process; and to Darcie Russell, whose insights, creative vision, and expertise added depth and quality to this book.

There are many individuals to whom I am grateful—for both their expertise and colleagueship. Their amazing work in areas such as school culture, learning communities, communication, collegiality, professional learning, brain research, change, leadership, and coaching provided a rich reservoir of knowledge from which to draw and inform my writings. Special thanks are due to Harvey Alvy, Cindy Bevevino, Mike Bossi, Mary Jane Boynton, Debbie Brown, Ashleigh Burnette, Patty Butz, R. Lynn Canady, Jeanie Cash, Ginny Connelly, Debbie and Lee Cooke, Ann Cunningham-Morris, D. D. Dawson, Terry Deal, Ann Delehant, Karen Dyer, Dot Earle, Maurice Elias, Debbie Estes, Carl Glickman, Jennifer Goss, Gayle Gregory, Tom Guskey, Mark Hansen, Cindy Harrison, Allen Haymon, Stephanie Hirsh, Bill Kennedy, Tara Kidwell, Joellen Killion, Karen Steinbrink Koch, Judith Warren Little, Judi Littman, Lou Martin, George Manthey, David Mathis, Kathleen McElroy, Ray McNulty, Jay McTighe, Caley Mikesell, Patrice Newnam, Kolia O'Connor, Kent Peterson, Jessica Riffey, Leah Roadcap, Leslie and Mike Rowland, Jane Scott, Renée Schuster, Dennis Sparks, Kelly

Tonsmeire, and Pat Wolfe. The late Claudia Gallant, Judy Arin Krupp, Gene Broderson, Gracia Alkema, Jane Bailey, Susan Loucks-Horsley, Frank Gomez, Loyd Wolfe, and Pat Schettini are gratefully remembered for their professional colleagueship, wisdom, and the profound difference they made in my life and the field of education.

Also deserving recognition are the wonderful peer coaches at Sewickley Academy's Lower School in Sewickley, Pennsylvania, a small town located just north and west of the city of Pittsburgh, and at Parkside Middle School in Prince William County, Virginia. Your commitment to education and willingness to engage in coaching, experiment with new ideas, learn, and share your knowledge and experiences are exemplary. Your dedication to making a difference has touched, and will continue to touch, many lives!

Introduction

While the world we live in is becoming ever more diverse, the common ground that connects all educators is an unwavering quest to improve professional practice in a way that enhances student performance. The specific names of programs may differ, but they focus on common topics: accountability; teacher evaluation; learning communities; data-driven decision making; science, technology, and engineering; arts; mathematics innovations; global education; differentiated instruction; 21st century learning skills; and school improvement. Each program has a laserlike focus on improving the depth of knowledge, skillfulness, resourcefulness, and inspiration of students and of those who educate them.

However, to quote Abraham Lincoln, "the situation is piled high with difficulty." As Linda Darling-Hammond (2013) explains, "Achieving these [reform-related] goals will require a transformation in teaching, learning, and assessment so that all students develop the deeper learning competencies that are necessary for post-secondary success." She emphasizes that addressing Common Core State Standards (CCSS) and other initiatives related to enhancing student performance will require even greater collaboration in schools, adding, "professionals benefit from connecting with dedicated colleagues to improve practice. What is surprising, even alarming, is how rarely collaborative activities that are essential for improving outcomes are supported by our schools." Reflecting on the roots of reform, Darling-Hammond notes, "The reform impulse that gave rise to the construction of new learning standards and assessments will only work if we invest in the capacity of educators to work together effectively." Peer Coaching provides the structures and processes to accomplish these important ends.

Much has changed in education since I wrote *How to Plan and Implement a Peer Coaching Program* (Robbins, 1991b). Classrooms have become more diverse, rich with many cultures and languages; the use of technology has advanced, with more tech-savvy professionals in our classrooms and schools; more is known about the science of teaching and learning—cognitive research, with its implications for practice, is more accessible; there is greater attention to the need to embed social and emotional learning into schools, given students' exposure to violence through social media, the news, and, sadly, even in their neighborhoods; there is greater emphasis on the need to differentiate learning experiences; there are national and international conversations about what students need to know and be able to do to thrive; many schools have expanded the value and use of teacher leadership; online resources for professional learning abound; and many schools have begun to realize the promise of operating as learning-focused, collaborative communities.

Nonetheless, many things in classrooms and schools have remained the same. Frequently, teachers still operate in isolation. In the privacy of their classrooms, these teachers often feel uncertain and have questions about practice, the curriculum, assessment, grading, and initiatives. Even if a school is moving toward collaborative work, years of isolation make some teachers tentative about getting involved. They wonder, "How do I measure up to other professionals in our school?" Or, feeling overwhelmed about all that they must do, they ponder, "Is it worth the investment of time?" Further, although advances in technology have enriched classroom learning environments, some teachers speak about how technology has precipitated isolation. As one teacher reflected,

> When we have a question, we can just Google it; when we need to talk to a colleague, we text or e-mail. It's so easy to use technology, and it helps us conserve time. As a consequence, we now

have fewer face-to-face forums and converse less about our practice and our students. We must remind ourselves of the value of our interactions, break out of isolation, and create time for connecting with one another.

As educators, we feel a sense of urgency to prepare our students to thrive. We have initiatives, research, and promising practices that illuminate the direction we must go to ensure that we accomplish this. However, context variables such as norms of isolation and lists of pressing demands make it difficult to focus daily attention on these. Ironically, these obstacles can actually be used as leverage points to begin the conversation about using professional collaboration to enhance the quality of learning experiences that students encounter.

Peer Coaching provides two types of structures for interactions—*collaborative work* and *formal coaching*—that can be implemented to address challenging initiatives, enact promising practices, and research informed strategies to build teachers' capacity to help every student to excel. When a school's culture includes a tradition of isolation and staff members are not yet comfortable with publicly sharing their craft knowledge, collaborative work offers several structures wherein teachers can collaborate without a classroom observation. These interactions can focus on topics of interest, such as the integrated use of technology in the curriculum. When trust, time, training, and tangible support for formal coaching exist, then peers can engage in a pre-conference, a classroom observation of a lesson, and a post-conference focused on teaching practices that enhance student learning.

Peer Coaching is a flexible strategy that can complement the implementation of pressing initiatives that aim to improve the quality of teaching and learning and professional and academic performance. Educators in one highly regarded school system, for example, have embraced Peer Coaching as a way to augment the quality and quantity of feedback to teachers about their instruction and its effect on student learning. Another district is using Peer Coaching to enhance the effectiveness of the implementation of CCSS; and yet another is using it to support the schoolwide implementation of *Understanding by Design* (Wiggins & McTighe, 2005). As these examples illustrate, Peer Coaching can leverage efforts to improve practice and performance in a variety of environments. Research suggests that in schools where teachers collaborate, academic achievement is four times more likely to improve than in schools where teachers work in isolation (Ann Lewis, quoted by Mike Schmoker, 2004). Well-functioning professional learning communities are experiencing these gains, often citing Peer Coaching as a valuable structure to promote learning-focused cultures of practice and teacher leadership, to articulate and integrate the curriculum, and to increase the use of promising practices across schools in order to meet the needs of every student.

Technology can enhance the Peer Coaching process, making it possible for individual teachers to see themselves teaching, as well as observe other exemplary teachers, even though release time may be scarce. For example, the Gates Foundation's Measures of Effective Teaching Project used technology so that teachers could observe themselves and others practicing their craft, asking challenging questions, and demonstrating multiple ways of explaining complex ideas. Teachers who had enhanced student outcomes reported that the videos, surveys, diagnostic tools, coaching, and collegial dialogue had a direct relationship to the results they achieved in the classroom. In addition, many teachers who are "flipping their classrooms"—for example, asking students to view video lectures at home so that more classroom time can be spent on discussion, questions, and projects—find Peer Coaching a helpful tool to compare and contrast their practices with those of other professionals. Digital cameras, Twitter, Facebook, Google Plus, Instagram, Skype, and blogs also add variety and value to opportunities to engage in dialogue about instructional practices and their effect on staff and student learning.

The movement toward greater accountability, with its emphasis on linking teacher evaluation to improved student achievement, is a noble one. However, many teacher evaluation efforts focus on assessing the presence or absence of desirable instructional or professional behaviors but fail to provide the support to develop these behaviors when they are ineffective or lacking. Peer Coaching offers a nonevaluative, differentiated, professional development support strategy so that teacher colleagues can plan lessons together; reflect together; have important discussions about curriculum, instruction, and assessment; observe lessons; and converse about the quality of assignments and student work; all with the goal of developing exemplary practices that leave their mark on staff and student learning. In other words, Peer Coaching represents the missing component in many efforts to enhance professional practice. It is a viable structure for job-embedded learning.

Using Peer Coaching structures to address important initiatives and enrich collegial interactions can foster meaningful, personalized professional growth for staff, magnify the influence of exemplary teaching, and augment the collective capacity of schools to provide responsive, high-quality learning experiences so that every student succeeds.

The chapters that follow will reveal what Peer Coaching is, how it works, and the critical role it can play in schools and other organizations to enhance professional practice and learning. The book will highlight key ingredients of successful Peer Coaching, identify possible pitfalls to be aware of when implementing it, and explain essential "how-to's" so that coaching work in literacy, math, science, social studies, and other areas can have a positive effect on classroom teaching and generate student learning.

The content of this book is rooted in both research and exemplary practices. It offers practical suggestions about how to get started; how to prepare the culture of the school; logistical considerations; coaching guidelines; considerations for communication (including difficult conversations); observation and conferencing strategies; the fit between coaching, mentoring, evaluation work, and other initiatives; and suggestions for professional development. It offers specific recommendations regarding how coaching can become an integral part of efforts to enhance learning and increase collaboration in schools, while building capacity and boosting morale. Throughout the chapters the voices of teachers and coaches will offer sage advice about implementing and supporting Peer Coaching efforts. At the end of each chapter is a set of reflective questions designed to deepen a reader's learning and to generate ideas for implementing the chapter's concepts in any workplace.

May the pages that follow offer guidance and inspiration that culminate in collaboration and learning!

1

Establishing the Need for Peer Coaching

Peer Coaching is a great tool for colleagues to use to help sharpen each other's skills. It is a way to get teachers out of the isolation of their classrooms and to really benefit from observing their colleagues in action. Not only does the process help the teacher being observed, but it also gives you a chance to learn a new style of teaching or to reinforce what you do with your students.

—Alison Howells, Spanish Teacher
Lower School, Sewickley Academy

Day in and day out, dedicated teachers work tirelessly in individual classrooms, many of them unassisted by coteachers or other professionals, focused on making a difference in the academic achievement and social-emotional learning of every child. More often than not, their students represent a wide array of learning differences in terms of skills, content knowledge, background experiences, interests, parental support, learning challenges, and self-confidence. They come from a variety of cultures and consequently view and speak about the world differently. Each one is trying to find his or her unique place in the world, and in school. Isolated in their classrooms, teachers often wonder, Did I use the best lesson strategy today to teach this standard? How would my colleague across the hall do it?

At the same time, most of the schools where these classrooms are located are reeling with changes in response to local, state, or federal initiatives, all with the expressed intent of enhancing teaching and learning: accountability, teacher evaluation, Common Core or state standards or benchmarks for performance, 21st century skills, preparing students to be college or career ready, new technologies, school improvement. The list is daunting. Within those same schools, principals, assistant principals, and other school leaders find themselves juggling these multiple initiatives while sensing the new classroom demands teachers are experiencing as a consequence. They want to support the work of individual teachers, yet they come up short when it comes to time. One suburban New Jersey principal shared this reflection:

> I am very much aware of the initiatives that face us. This reality is juxtaposed with the fact that our school population changed dramatically this year as a result of redistricting. Our new boundary lines have brought a significant number of students to our school from war-torn nations, some of them never having attended school before. We also have a growing number of students who are homeless. Our entire faculty is scrambling to discover the practices we need to address the new composition of our student body. We can't do it alone; we need each other. To some extent, we will be able to use our existing grade-level and subject-area-specific professional learning communities to find answers to the new challenges, but I also want to be able to increase the opportunity each faculty member has to receive feedback about their teaching practices and student learning, as well as have the opportunity to grow professionally. That is why we are developing a Peer Coaching program. (Personal communication, August 2014)

Peer Coaching offers several vibrant structures for collegial interactions to address important initiatives. It also fosters meaningful, personalized, professional growth opportunities for staff; increases the influence of exemplary teaching; and magnifies the collective propensity of schools to be able to provide responsive, high-quality learning experiences to ensure that every student succeeds.

A Definition of Peer Coaching

Peer Coaching is a powerful, confidential, nonevaluative process through which two or more colleagues work together to do the following:

- Reflect upon and analyze teaching practices and their consequences
- Develop and articulate curriculum
- Create informal assessments to measure student learning
- Implement new instructional strategies, including the integrated use of technology
- Plan lessons collaboratively
- Discuss student assessment data and plan for future learning experiences
- Expand, refine, and build new skills
- Share ideas and resources
- Teach one another
- Conduct classroom research
- Solve classroom problems or address workplace challenges
- Examine and study student learning with the goal of improving professional practice to maximize student success

Purposes and Forms of Peer Coaching

Schools around the world have implemented Peer Coaching programs for a variety of purposes. For example, Peer Coaching has been used to augment the availability of feedback to teachers about teaching and learning; to increase problem-solving capabilities; to build teachers' capacity to address new standards, benchmarks, or CCSS; to support teachers in planning instructional time within a block schedule; to expand the integrated use of technology; to develop teachers' content-area expertise; to design challenging student work; to refine teachers' instructional repertoire and competencies in an instructional framework; and to personalize professional learning. It is essential that the purpose of Peer Coaching reflect the needs and aspirations of the individuals who will be engaged in it.

Trust must be present in order to have meaningful conversations about practice. Trusting relationships among professional colleagues are often the missing ingredient needed to sustain Peer Coaching success. For instance, in the United States and abroad, many literacy and math coaches are failing in their efforts to change instructional practice and promote learning because, although they have exceptional content-area knowledge, they are not taking the time to focus on the meaningful underpinnings (relationship building and trust) that are a requisite part of results-oriented coaching.

Peer Coaching activities are as individual and unique as the people who participate in them. As noted in the Introduction, Peer Coaching activities fall into two broad categories. The first category, *collaborative work*, engages professional colleagues in using collaborative structures to increase their capacity to promote learning; these structures are not tied to classroom observations. The second category, *formal coaching*, occurs within a classroom and usually includes a pre-conference, an observation, and a post-conference. For instance, multiple colleagues from one department may be engaged in *collaborative work* focused on aligning curriculum with CCSS, developing common assessments, or analyzing student work. In another context, two colleagues may be involved with *formal coaching* that includes a conversation about a lesson plan, an observation of that lesson, and reflecting on the lesson and the student work it produced.

As these examples illustrate, the variety of forms Peer Coaching can take are limitless. Generally speaking, Peer Coaching activities change in form and structure as relationships among colleagues grow more trusting and comfortable, and as need dictates. If trust is just beginning to develop, staff members may initially prefer to work collegially outside the classroom. For example, teachers may study "mathematical shifts" related to CCSS in a small forum led by a math coach or facilitated by another teacher. Then groups of colleagues may view online videos of exemplary CCSS math lessons and dialogue about the teaching practices they observed and the resulting student performance. Next, as trust develops, professional colleagues may draw from these prior learning experiences and create math lessons together, incorporating the mathematical shifts, teaching strategies, assignments for student work, and assessments that are appropriate, given the instructional outcomes, performance data, and levels of student achievement and understanding in a class. Finally, teachers may form pairs or trios so that one teacher can teach the lesson they helped develop, while the others observe. Following the lesson, the teacher and observers may reflect and analyze what led to desirable student performance and what they might do differently. Under some circumstances, the teacher and observers may revise the lesson. One of the observers then teaches the revised lesson to a different group of students, while the teacher who taught the previous lesson becomes an observer. At the conclusion of the lesson, teacher and observers meet to reflect on the teaching experiences from both lessons, as well as student performance, and generate recommendations for practices that have a high probability of fostering student learning. Over time, these types of activities create job-embedded professional learning experiences that fuel the staff's capacity to serve students as they simultaneously implement challenging initiatives.

Using Peer Coaching to Address Challenges and Opportunities

Peer Coaching has the potential to bring opportunities, as well as the potential to address many of the challenges that educators face, including some related to the widespread use of technology. One teacher described the situation in this way:

> We are at the "island stage." Because our faculty room was moved to a different floor, we often text or e-mail each other rather than make the trip upstairs—especially in a time crunch. So we have become isolated from face-to-face interactions. Peer Coaching will afford an opportunity to have another set of eyes in our classrooms.

In this case, technology can also be a helpful tool, by capturing—visually and auditorily—teachers' interactions with students and providing a medium through which they can examine those interactions and their consequences with a trusted colleague. For example, Videre (Manthey & Cash, 2014) is an iPad application that teachers have used to record teaching episodes. Colleagues review and categorize what they have recorded, labeling sections that they want to revisit and discuss. Describing her experience, one Northern California teacher reflected,

> I was interested in how I incorporate questions that require critical or creative thinking throughout a lesson, and I wondered which students I called on to answer these questions. My coach used Videre to record my interactions and labeled selected portions "critical thinking," "creative thinking," and "student responses." When we conferenced after the lesson, we were able to go right to these lesson segments to discuss them. It was a real time-saver.

Technology has also played a significant role, answering needs as schools face reduced budgets for release time using substitute teachers and as a way to accommodate the many teachers who have after-school commitments or demands at home. For example, when schedules or budgets prohibit releasing teachers to observe colleagues, many teachers have used digital video cameras and smartphones to record themselves, and then they meet with colleagues via Skype in the evenings, from their homes.

Peer coaches can also focus observations on the classroom use of technology to increase student engagement. By focusing an observation on the use of technology, teachers have the opportunity to review the desired lesson outcomes during the pre-conference and talk about how technology will be used as a medium for students' active involvement. During the observation, the observer collects data about what students are doing and how technology played a part in facilitating active participation. In the post-conference, the teacher is invited to reflect on what happened during the lesson, converse about what modifications might be made, and analyze whether the use of technology helped students to master the intended outcomes.

Preparing students to be college or career ready is another challenge that can engage Peer Coaches. In one Wisconsin district, Peer Coaching partners studied the research on the skills necessary to succeed. After compiling the data, they examined both curriculum areas and classroom processes in which they could meaningfully and authentically embed these skills. Then they developed lessons together in which they embedded the skills, taught the lessons, analyzed the resulting student work, and used the data to inform future lessons. One teacher reflected on the coaching work this focus entailed as follows:

> Critical and creative thinking were 21st century skills we sought to impart to our students. We actually had to think critically and creatively to accomplish this goal. Hence, we had the opportunity to strengthen our capacity as professional colleagues in the quest to serve students. Peer Coaching provided the medium to accomplish this.

Today's classrooms are more diverse and more inclusive with respect to language, cultures, skills, and knowledge than ever before. Teachers find themselves pressured to help every student meet rigorous, standardized learning targets within a specified length of time. At one middle school in Ohio, Peer Coaching colleagues decided to address the challenges of diversity by forming a book club and reading *The Differentiated Classroom: Responding to the Needs of All Learners* by Carol Ann Tomlinson (2014). One teacher explained how the book inspired colleagues to design differentiated lessons for their students:

> Resources in the book gave us the strategies we needed to coplan lessons for diverse learners. Using the lessons we had developed, one of us taught, while the other observed. Then we conferenced about the impact of the use of these strategies on student learning. This coaching work increased our skill sets and the facility with which we delivered instruction and generated treasured results—student learning!

As schools seek to reinvent themselves so that they can prepare students to thrive, many are reorganizing their use of time. In a Connecticut high school that transitioned to a block schedule consisting of 90-minute periods, teachers used Peer Coaching activities to examine effective teaching strategies for the block schedule and to coplan interdisciplinary lessons. Following a workshop based on *Thinking Inside the Block Schedule: Strategies for Teaching in Extended Periods of Time* (Robbins, Gregory, & Herndon, 2000), teachers organized Peer Coaching cadres by departments and began "chunking the curriculum." Then they began coplanning lessons in which they integrated instructional strategies they had learned in the workshop, as well as interdisciplinary concepts. After working together to develop the lessons, one teacher committed to functioning as coach, while the other served as teacher. Together, they participated in a pre-conference, a lesson observation, and a post-conference. Afterward, one of the department heads noted,

> Peer Coaching allowed us to build our repertoire of teaching strategies for the block schedule, enhanced our collaboration as department members, and increased our work across departments. Collectively, this helped us grow as professional colleagues and ultimately resulted in raising student achievement.

Teacher accountability is another trend. Charlotte Danielson writes,

> Virtually every state requires observations of teaching as a significant contributor to high-stakes judgments about teacher quality. To be defensible, the systems that yield these observations must have clear standards of practice, instruments and procedures through which teachers can demonstrate their skill, and trained and certified observers who can make accurate and consistent judgments based on evidence.

> In addition, it's possible to design approaches to classroom observation that yield important learning for teachers by incorporating practices associated with professional learning—namely, self-assessment, reflection on practice, and professional conversation.

When these practices are put in place, classroom observation can make a dramatic contribution to the culture of a school. (2012, p. 37)

Many districts are seizing the opportunity to implement Peer Coaching in response to this movement—not as an extension of evaluation, but rather as a tool for professional learning, focused on developing a vision of effective instruction, creating a common language of practice, constructing an avenue for building competence in specific domains, and, in the process of doing this, generating norms of continuous improvement within a culture committed to fostering learning for every one of its members.

Kolia O'Connor, Head of School at Sewickley Academy, astutely explains how Peer Coaching enriches the professional practice of teachers and the quality of learning experiences that students encounter, while informing and strengthening the collegial and student-focused community that characterizes exemplary schools. His valuable insights can be found in Appendix A.

As these examples illustrate, Peer Coaching can accelerate the implementation of initiatives designed to enhance the use of technology, address challenges associated with CCSS, differentiate instruction, support implementation of new schedules, boost teacher effectiveness, deepen subject-area expertise, improve staff relationships, build a more learning-focused, collaborative culture, and enhance student learning.

Voluntary or Mandatory?

Ideally, Peer Coaching activities are voluntary. However, in some settings, principals and other school leaders have decided that they would like all staff members to be exposed to coaching so that they may experience its benefits. In some schools, principals have chosen to support Peer Coaching because of its value in providing nonjudgmental feedback to teachers who were not going to be formally evaluated, and because it serves as an additional source of feedback to those who were going to be formally evaluated. Although in many cases the "exposure" to coaching was initially a source of stress and was often accompanied by doubt, most teachers came to warmly embrace Peer Coaching. Carol McCormish, a 5th grade teacher at Sewickley Academy in Pennsylvania reflects as follows:

> When I was first approached to participate in a Peer Coaching workshop, I had my doubts about its effectiveness. My initial thought was "we are now going to be evaluating our colleagues and our observations are going to be used for compensation purposes." As I learned more about the program, I realized Peer Coaching was a method to enhance my teaching and to direct my observers to the areas that I wished to have more information about. From observing my movements in the room, to watching the behaviors of one or two of my students, to documenting the progression of my lesson, the feedback was not only eye-opening but helped me to redirect my thinking when designing my lessons, making each lesson more effective.

Dr. Mary Jane Boynton, principal of Parkside Middle School in Prince William County, Virginia, explained her rationale for integrating Peer Coaching as a part of professional learning at the school:

> I wanted to offer Peer Coaching to the staff at Parkside as a way to enrich the collaborative peer interactions they were already having, while also providing teachers the opportunity to learn from one another. Additionally, since we had moved into a shared leadership model and more of the staff were becoming teacher leaders, Peer Coaching was the natural next step. Peer Coaching provided the teacher leaders with further opportunities to support our students at Parkside while also providing support, strategies, resources, and different perspectives to many of the teachers who may not reach out for enrichment in other forums...

> Peer Coaching is a long-term investment. It requires financial resources to provide the training and the time for the Peer Coaching sessions, as well as the substitute teachers to facilitate the

release time so that conferencing and observations can occur. It is imperative that peer coaches have trust with their colleagues. It is essential that staff members understand and believe that this is not just an unofficial form of teacher evaluation. All in all, our experience has been positive. The journey has been slow, but for the teachers who have taken the training, they are excited and ready to continue this next year.

In Illinois, Community Consolidated School District 181 used Peer Coaching districtwide to "integrate the implementation of the Common Core standards with the district's curriculum renewal cycle, school improvement plans, and recommendations from a program evaluation of our gifted and talented program," explained district superintendent Dr. Renée Schuster. She continued with the following remarks:

> Our Department of Learning researched different approaches to coaching and decided to focus our professional development on Peer Coaching because we wanted to create a culture of coaching built upon collaboration through which all staff learn together and share their expertise. In 2013–2014, we began Peer Coaching with a year of professional development in which teams from every school participated in monthly full-day sessions… We perceived several outcomes from the implementation of Peer Coaching:
>
> 1. Increased conversation about improving teaching and learning
> 2. Increased collaboration among teams within and across schools
> 3. Increased understanding of the school improvement process
> 4. Increased consistency in the implementation of reading and writing workshop[s]
> 5. Increased understanding of the new Illinois Standards Incorporating the Common Core

Appendix A contains an expanded commentary about District 181's experiences with Peer Coaching.

The Principal's Role in Peer Coaching

Principals play a vital role in determining the success or failure of Peer Coaching, and they demonstrate support in a variety of ways. They communicate the value of Peer Coaching by speaking about it as a vibrant part of the culture; allocating time and other resources for coaching; promoting schoolwide norms, such as risk taking, that reinforce the spirit of coaching; creating line-item budget allocations for coaching; reserving prime time on faculty-meeting agendas for discussing coaching activities and experiences; and championing its importance with central office personnel, board members, parents, community members, staff, and students.

Principals also model their philosophical support for coaching by collaborating with teachers and demonstrating the Peer Coaching process, explicitly articulating that there is no connection between Peer Coaching and evaluation, substituting for teachers so that they can coach their peers, coordinating schedules and substitutes for coaching interactions, sharing research and exemplary practices about Peer Coaching, and occasionally, if invited by a teacher, functioning as coach or "the teacher to be observed." In one high school, the principal asked the assistant principal and a teacher-leader to coach her as she planned, delivered, and reflected upon a faculty meeting. The pre-conference was conducted in front of the faculty before the beginning of the meeting. During the meeting, the assistant principal and the teacher-leader collected observational data that the principal had requested at the pre-conference. Finally, a post-conference was conducted at the conclusion of the faculty meeting and the principal publicly reflected about the insights she gained as a result of the Peer Coaching process. Asked why she did this, she responded, "I'd never ask faculty members to do anything that I would not do myself." Such participation adds credibility to Peer Coaching and increases the principal's awareness of the demands of coaching.

Why Would a Principal Want Peer Coaching in a School?

For principals and staff interested in building a collaborative culture, Peer Coaching has the potential to promote several positive outcomes. It offers a process through which teachers can be empowered to take on new leadership roles within the school. Enhanced collaboration among teachers can promote an articulated curriculum aligned with valued standards and benchmarks; provide increased opportunities for interdisciplinary planning and units to prepare college- or career-ready students; support the integrated use of technology; and offer an opportunity to tap the otherwise well-kept secrets of practice, or "craft knowledge," hidden away in individual classrooms. Teachers benefit by feeling less isolated and having a greater support system with multiple resources for curriculum, instruction, assessment, student work, and problem solving. Teachers often become one another's teachers because of the collaborative structures; hence, their practices are informed less by trial and error. Teachers build a shared knowledge base about teaching and learning, accessible to novices and veterans alike. Their collaborative work introduces new structures into the school culture, as well as norms that support risk taking and experimentation. Peer Coaching offers the principal a way to differentiate and extend the feedback available to teachers by creating several structures—separate from supervision and evaluation—through which teachers can view themselves, their classroom work, and the visible learning their teaching produces.

Collectively, Peer Coaching activities focus attention on the quality of teaching and learning in a school, as well as the avenues for professional growth and development. In this respect, Peer Coaching structures and functions build what Roland Barth (1990) refers to as a "community of learners" committed to the lifelong learning of every member of the school organization.

Dr. Harvey Alvy, former teacher and principal, founding member of the Principals' Training Center for International Schools, National NAESP Distinguished Principal for Overseas Schools, and Professor Emeritus at Eastern Washington University, was asked to respond to the question "Why did you value Peer Coaching when you were principal?" He thoughtfully replied as follows:

> Peer Coaching helped to define and shape our school culture. Peer Coaching provided faculty with a forum to live their values. When engaging in Peer Coaching, faculty were modeling life-long learning for each other, and for our students. When teachers decided on Peer Coaching topics and observed the classrooms of colleagues, students observed teachers learning from each other.
>
> Teaching and learning are very complex actions. Unless individuals are willing to grow and learn, it is impossible to remain on the cutting edge of the teaching profession. As a principal, I knew that whenever teachers were having Peer Coaching conversations, they were getting feedback on their work and accomplishing goals that paralleled the work I pursued when engaging in personalized supervisory activities. Also, by observing and visiting teacher peers, faculty helped to "lower the temperature" when administrators visited classrooms for evaluative purposes. The classrooms were no longer isolated spaces—they were welcoming places for everyone interested in teaching and learning.
>
> As Peer Coaching teams became more comfortable with their work, and as trust increased, the variety of professional development activities expanded. Interestingly, this gave me an opportunity to support and facilitate other capacity-building activities that they brought to my attention. I could provide the space as well as fiscal and material resources. However, they decided whether to tackle a schoolwide teaching, curriculum, or assessment issue. They decided on whether to address a grade-level, subject-area, or idiosyncratic need. This was incredibly powerful—outside forces were not making professional development decisions that affected their everyday work. Teachers were making the decisions. Teacher leadership became the rule, not the exception. And, at the end of the day, as a school principal, I firmly believed that as teachers grow, students grow.

Closing Thoughts

Superintendent Renée Schuster reflected that

> Peer Coaching takes time, and you will experience successes and
> challenges along the way. Expect mid-course adjustments, for this
> is the synergy that comes from the coaching process and is the
> origin of some of our best ideas. Finally, kindness, encourage-
> ment, and respect go a long way in fostering a culture of coach-
> ing. (Personal communication, July 2014)

Summary

Peer Coaching is a nonevaluative process in which two or more colleagues work together on various aspects of teaching, such as analyzing
instructional practices, planning lessons, expanding or refining skills,
and implementing new strategies. It can serve many purposes, including providing additional feedback to teachers about their instruction,
increasing their capacity to address new standards and initiatives,
developing their content-area expertise, and helping them to design
challenging student work. Two broad categories of Peer Coaching are
collaborative work, which involves out-of-classroom professional interactions focused on teaching and learning, and *formal coaching*, which
often involves a pre-conference, an observation, and a post-conference.
Both categories require trusting relationships as their foundation. Peer
Coaching has been implemented to address a variety of challenges
and opportunities, including those related to technology, increased
diversity in the classroom, ensuring that students are college or career
ready, block scheduling and other changes in how time is organized,
and teacher accountability. Ideally, Peer Coaching is a voluntary
job-embedded learning strategy. However, in some schools it has been
implemented as a mandate. Regardless of whether Peer Coaching is
voluntary or mandatory, the principal plays a vital role in supporting
implementation. Principals may promote Peer Coaching for various

reasons, including empowering teachers to take on new leadership roles, improving interdisciplinary planning, and enhancing the implementation of learning initiatives. In all cases, the ultimate goal is improved staff and student learning. In Chapter 2, the forms that Peer Coaching can take are explored.

Reflective Questions

1. What are your thoughts about the definition of Peer Coaching presented in this chapter? Is there anything you would change or modify about it?

2. Which of the initiatives being implemented in your workplace are presenting the greatest challenges? Why?

3. How might collaborative work or formal coaching activities support implementation of the initiatives being addressed?

4. Thinking about your school's student performance data, which areas indicate a need for focus? Would collaborative work or formal coaching activities be useful to address these areas? Why or why not?

5. How might Peer Coaching provide opportunities for professional growth and teacher leadership in your school?

2

Exploring the Forms
of Peer Coaching

For me, the best part of Peer Coaching was having my colleagues "see my world," and I certainly enjoyed seeing theirs. Teaching can be a very isolating profession since we teach in separate rooms, on varying schedules, and teach different subject areas. I liked hearing the language my peers used in their classrooms, and seeing how some of my students responded in a different environment. Observing someone else teach and commenting on it at first felt a bit judgmental, but when we focused only on communicating on what the teacher wanted us to provide feedback about, I think it ended up being beneficial and affirmative. I liked knowing what others noticed about my instructional delivery and appreciated the "observation-informed input" from those who seemed to understand the "why" behind what I was trying to accomplish with my students. I think it is important to have your peers be people you like and respect so that the interactions remain positive.

—Sally Weir, Reading Specialist
Lower School, Sewickley Academy

All Peer Coaching activities share a common, collaborative quest to refine, expand, and enhance knowledge about the teaching profession in ways that leave a mark on practice; build a more collaborative, learning-focused culture; enhance the resources available for problem solving; and increase the quality of students' learning experiences, resulting in higher levels of student achievement. As discussed in Chapter 1, Peer Coaching activities fall into two categories: collaborative work and formal coaching. Figure 2.1 depicts the types of collaborative work that build the trust necessary to support formal coaching roles. Typically, if trust among professional colleagues is not well developed, coaching efforts should begin with collaborative work. Once trust is established, colleagues are more comfortable being observed by a colleague. In many settings where trust exists, colleagues engage in collaborative work as well as formal coaching. In the paragraphs that follow, an overview of collaborative work and formal coaching is provided.

FIGURE 2.1

Examining Collaborative Work and Peer Coaching Roles

Peer Coaching can encompass many structures, roles, and activities. Collaborative Work often serves to build readiness for formal coaching roles, though individuals engaged in Formal Coaching Roles may also participate in Collaborative Work.

Collaborative Work

- Sharing stories about teaching practices
- Analyzing videos of teaching practices
- Solving problems of professional practice
- Implementing study groups
- Having conversations focused on student work
- Participating in book talks
- Participating in data talks
- Coplanning lessons

Formal Coaching Roles

- Coteach one or more lessons
- Act as collaborator
- Serve as expert advisor
- Act as a mentor
- Serve as a mirror
- Provide professional learning resources

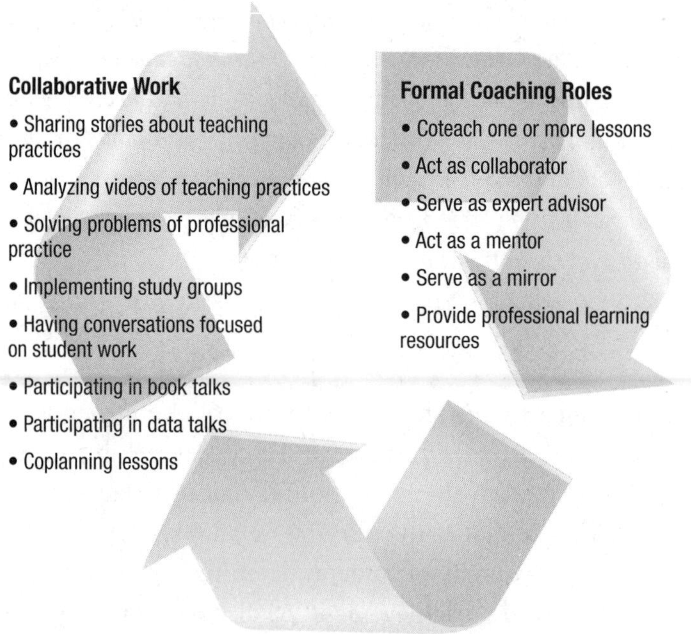

Collaborative Work

Collaborative work engages two or more professional colleagues, or sometimes groups or teams, in informal interactions, usually structured to reflect a specific focus, independent of a classroom observation. For example, collaborative work may focus on instructional strategies, curriculum, CCSS, assessment, use of time, classroom procedures and routines, specific students, inclusion practices, working with English language learners, student work, strategies to meaningfully integrate technology, or critical and creative thinking. Or the work may focus on implementing a particular initiative, such as in the examples discussed in Chapter 1. Collaborative work activities may occur within the classroom, teachers' workroom, grade level, department, professional learning community (PLC) team meeting, faculty meeting, virtual meeting, or professional development session. Activities may engage professional colleagues in face-to-face interactions or connect them electronically via social media.

Many teachers doing collaborative work have indicated that when trust is developing and teachers are not yet comfortable having a colleague observe their teaching, opportunities to collaborate outside the classroom provide a chance to do learning-focused work while building trust, but in a fear-free environment. One veteran teacher of 15 years explained,

> My only experience being observed in the first 10 years of teaching was when the principal did walkthroughs or a formal evaluation visit. Initially, because of this prior evaluation experience, I was reluctant to have a peer watch me practice my craft. Instead, I found comfort in meeting with a colleague who I called my thought partner, problem solving the learning challenges of specific students, and then coplanning lessons for those students. Eventually, these out-of-classroom activities created the trust and rapport that enabled me to feel comfortable inviting my thought partner into my classroom to observe me, and then I went into her classroom to observe her. Building the foundation of trust

and rapport first created a much needed comfort for meaningful conversations focused on teaching and learning. (Personal communication, June 2014)

Specific collaborative work activities, such as those listed in Figure 2.1 (e.g., video analysis, problem solving, study groups) are described in greater detail in Chapter 3; but for now, it is important to note that taking the time to engage in learning-focused collaborative work is essential for building the foundational underpinnings requisite for productive formal coaching. When time is not invested to build trust, relationships, and understanding by doing collaborative work, more often than not formal coaching efforts are superficial and short-lived.

Formal Coaching

Formal coaching takes place within the classroom and, with the exception of coteaching, usually involves a pre-conference, an observation, and a post-conference. Most often the *inviting teacher*—the person who issues the invitation to the coach—decides on the focus, which is usually directed toward examining a teaching practice that affects student learning. Formal coaching can engage two or three teachers, or, in some cases, a team. Coaching may occur between experienced teachers, an expert and a novice, or experienced and less experienced teachers. Reflecting on the multiple forms of formal coaching in which she has participated in her career, Ann Robertson, math chair at Parkside Middle School, said, "I never thought I was too young to be better, or too tenured to become more masterful. This process can only aid you, and aid the team, making us stronger. In the end, it benefits our students tremendously."

Approaches to formal coaching vary. One type is designed to help teachers transfer the new skills they have learned in a workshop or training session into classroom practice. This type of coaching usually follows training in specific strategies or methods. For instance, if the training has addressed the elements of a lesson strategy such as concept attainment, participants would learn the theory supporting concept attainment, observe a demonstration of its use, practice the strategy, and receive feedback in their use of the strategy within the training session. The coaching process would revolve around how the teacher is implementing the strategy in the classroom. Teachers pair with consultants or with one another so that they can receive feedback about the application of the new strategy in the classroom. The focus of Peer Coaching activities in this context is directly related to the workshop or training content. Research has shown that this approach promotes skill transfer. Joyce and Showers (1982) assert, "Like athletes, teachers will put newly learned skills to use—if they are coached" (p. 5). Another variable affecting implementation of newly learned skills is whether an individual values the skill or sees a need for it in classroom practice. Taking time to explore examples of how a strategy might be used and its consequences, in terms of student learning, is essential during professional development sessions and later, during job-embedded coaching experiences.

If this is the only type of formal coaching that teachers experience, however, the process may become routine and the coaching may turn into coaching as unreflective practice (Hargreaves, 1989), wherein teachers simply go through the motions of labeling the implemented behaviors and consequences. When this happens, the aspects of the lesson that the teacher is genuinely curious about may go unaddressed (Robbins, 1984). To be effective and sustained over time, coaching activities must not only have a deliberate focus, but that focus must be one that matters to the individuals involved.

Other approaches to formal coaching involve colleagues working together around issues unrelated to a focus generated by shared training. This type of formal coaching relies on a teacher-specified focus. Here the approach is intended to increase reflective practice, teaching repertoire, and resourcefulness, with the ultimate goal being increased student learning. In one school that was implementing an iPad initiative, the teachers decided to focus formal coaching efforts on how pairs of students could use teacher-designed practice tasks to increase mastery of the concepts they were teaching, while building students' skillfulness in collaborative work. One teacher had extensive experience in this area and served as an expert advisor to his colleagues, modeling how one could use the iPad for projects to actively engage pairs of students, spark creativity, and bring history alive.

In other schools, formal coaching has involved conducting action research, solving problems related to instruction or curriculum design and delivery, and addressing learning challenges encountered by specific students.

Formal coaching can also include "mentor coaching," which Nolan (2007) defines as a "structured process whereby an experienced person introduces, assists, and supports a less-experienced person (the protégé) in a personal and professional growth process" (p. 3). Coaches who serve as mentors provide valuable induction experiences for beginning teachers in ways that help the novices become more self-reliant and skillful. As a result of the mentor's coaching, the newcomer learns how to plan comprehensively, select appropriate teaching strategies that will engage learners, monitor and adjust instruction based on the learners' performance, assess the learning, and plan for the next instructional steps.

Sometimes when teachers just want to "see and hear" their own classroom, a coach can function as a mirror—recording or scripting classroom interactions so that the teacher can review these after teaching a lesson.

Peer Coaching Roles

Just as Peer Coaching activities vary widely, the roles coaches play in fulfilling coaching commitments differ as well. Joellen Killion and Cindy Harrison (2006) describe 10 different roles coaches fill in their work, explaining that some coaches play out all of these, while others have a more narrow focus, serving in only a few. Killion (2009) notes that the roles "constitute a range of support coaches provide teachers. Each role requires a specific set of knowledge and skills. Each role has a distinctive set of challenges. Each meets a specific teacher need" (p. 9). The coaching roles that Killion and Harrison identify include data coach, resource provider, mentor, curriculum specialist, instructional specialist, classroom supporter, learning facilitator, school leader, catalyst for change, and learner. Which roles a coach plays are determined by a number of factors. These include "coaches' job descriptions, their role expectations, the goals of the coaching program, the goals of a school's improvement plan, the context in which they work, the time of the school year, the experience of the coach and the experience of the teacher" (Killion, 2009, p. 14).

Regardless of the form or approach, the common thread that runs through every coaching activity is that it connects professional colleagues and provides resources in ways that ultimately enhance the quality of the learning opportunities that students experience. The result? Refined teaching practices, augmented resources, teacher learning, and student success. Further, the context in which these activities take place becomes more collaborative and learning focused—creating bridges that foster communication between and among professional colleagues. Although coaching activities, if voluntary, may involve only segments of a school staff, collectively they can increase the climate of collegiality *if they become an integral part of life at the school and if the school culture provides a hospitable environment.*

Factors That Influence the Success of Peer Coaching

The context in which Peer Coaching interactions occur has a profound effect on the success of implementation. Figure 2.2 (p. 30) illustrates the foundation and pillars of support necessary for a vibrant Peer Coaching process.

Taking time to assess contextual variables to determine if work must be done to cultivate the culture and climate of the organization, school, or department in which Peer Coaching is to be implemented will help ensure that coaching efforts thrive. To create an environment that supports Peer Coaching, there must be a shared belief that every

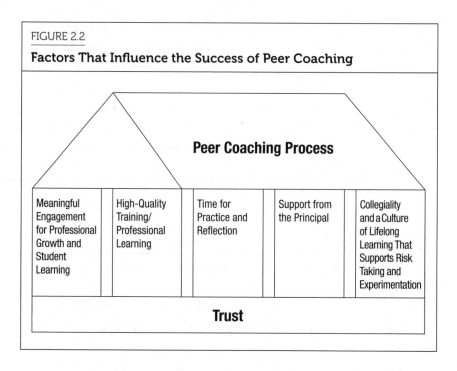

FIGURE 2.2

Factors That Influence the Success of Peer Coaching

Peer Coaching Process

| Meaningful Engagement for Professional Growth and Student Learning | High-Quality Training/ Professional Learning | Time for Practice and Reflection | Support from the Principal | Collegiality and a Culture of Lifelong Learning That Supports Risk Taking and Experimentation |

Trust

person has the capacity to grow professionally. Every individual must have a sense of psychological and emotional safety. The words of veteran teacher and math department chair Ann Robertson reflect the mindset teachers need:

> I consider myself a lifelong learner, and no matter how many years of experience one has, every educator can always improve one's craft or expertise. Students, methods, practices, and current research are constantly changing what we have learned in the classroom. My involvement has been to make best practices better and bring a sense of camaraderie to those with whom I work. Engagement in Peer Coaching provides a way to be honest with ourselves and yet feel comfortable making our teaching better, not just to benefit ourselves, but rather to benefit those we touch daily.

One major factor in creating a nurturing environment for Peer Coaching is building a climate of trust in which risk taking and experimentation can occur. Trust becomes the foundation for all Peer Coaching interactions. Bryk and Schneider (2004) note that school staffs characterized by relational trust among professional colleagues are more likely to take risks and make the kinds of changes that result in student achievement. Peer Coaching will, at times, invite new ideas, new behaviors, new materials, and new ways of operating. People need a safe environment to feel comfortable embarking on a journey of exploring and examining their practices and the consequences of those practices.

The classic work of Costa and Garmston (2002) in Cognitive Coaching identifies three areas in which a coach must build trust: *in self, between individuals, and in the coaching process*. Trust in self involves having a clear sense of our own values and beliefs. Being consistent, open, accessible, nonjudgmental, and able to admit our mistakes are all characteristics of trust in ourselves. When reflecting on their practices, teachers must adopt a stance of objectivity. This stance will ensure that data collection will not be obscured by bias and Peer Coaching artifacts such as videos, portfolios, journals, and observation notes will be judgment free. Raising an awareness of the lenses through which we look at ourselves, our colleagues, and our work can be a valuable leadership and coaching tool. Some coaches and school leaders take assessments to identify their personality "style" to increase their awareness of how it may influence what they value and how they record data during observations.

Relational trust among professional colleagues is a must for coaching efforts to be authentic and useful. Trust between and among teachers and coaches develops over time as individuals' actions align with their words, and as they learn what is important to those with whom they work, come to understand how others process information, and become aware of their colleagues' personalities, thoughts, and concerns.

Observing norms of confidentiality is another aspect of the trust-building process. Knowing that a colleague commits to keeping conversations and observations confidential (as long as students are not being harmed, of course) creates a safe space where thoughts, ideas, and concerns can be aired without fear of criticism.

For Peer Coaching to endure over time and become institutional-ized as a viable source of job-embedded professional learning, teachers must trust in the Peer Coaching process. This entails believing that collaborative work and formal coaching activities are intended to be learning focused, with the goals of adding to the professional reper-toire of staff, refining teaching practices, augmenting the collective resources of staff members to serve students, expanding problem-solv-ing capabilities, enhancing expertise, and building a collaborative, pro-fessional culture of learning dedicated to helping every student thrive. Trust deepens as individuals involved in coaching activities feel safe and become assured that the process is not connected in any way to teacher evaluation. Absence of threat is a vital ingredient in cultivating an environment where Peer Coaching thrives.

Another critical element is trust and respect among teachers and administrators. Blase and Blase (2000) suggest that for teachers and administrators to develop trusting relationships, they must

- Listen with respect;
- Be a model of trust;
- Help others communicate effectively;
- Clarify expectations;
- Celebrate experimentation and support risk taking; and
- Exhibit personal integrity. (p. 36)

Principals and other school leaders can convey their support for Peer Coaching in various ways. These include creating opportunities for training in Peer Coaching; allocating time for teachers to practice coaching skills; scheduling time for coaching to take place on a regular basis; allocating resources such as quality substitute teachers to cover classrooms while teachers coach or while pre-conferences, observa-tions, and post-conferences are conducted; and building a professional library about coaching and related topics such as communication, observation tools, personality styles, and leadership. Clutterbuck (2005), cited in Zepeda (2012), lists the following indicators of an organizational climate that supports coaching:

• Personal growth, team development, and organizational learning are integrated and the links clearly understood;
• People are able to engage in constructive and positive confrontation;
• People welcome feedback (even at the top) and actively seek it;
• Coaching is seen as a joint responsibility;
• Coaching is seen primarily as an opportunity rather than as a remedial intervention;
• Time for reflection is valued; and
• There are effective mechanisms for identifying and addressing barriers to learning. (p. 175)

For Peer Coaching to succeed, risk taking, experimentation, voicing conflicting opinions, and resistance are actually essential. These actions thrive in an environment characterized by trust and safety. Hence, a vital first step for creating a successful Peer Coaching program is attending to how to develop such an atmosphere. Konni de Goeij (2013) states

How change and trust building will be addressed at a school site depends on such issues as a school's history, student diversity, staff turnover, relationships among staff members, schedules and logistics, and degree of community support… The role of principal is critical in establishing and maintaining trust. Indeed, the ability to trust in one's own working environment and to contribute in a trusting and open manner have emerged as important facets of healthy school environments. (p. 99)

It is also important to note that in some schools and organizations, collaboration has not been a workplace norm. In these contexts, because Peer Coaching requires new forms of working relationships among individuals, greater attention is first devoted to building relationships, with less attention on a specific end, such as achievement. As a result, performance may decrease initially (Robbins, 1991a). Fullan and Miles (1992) describe this experience as the implementation dip: "Even in cases where reform eventually succeeds, things often go wrong before they go right" (p. 749). Therefore, trust—among individuals and within the culture of the school—is an essential ingredient in the change process. Leaders build trust by promoting "a school culture that emphasizes cooperation and caring, rather than competition and favoritism" (Uebbing & Ford, 2011).

Because new ways of thinking and new practices require people to learn or relearn—and because first attempts are often less than perfect—failure, resistance, and disappointment are predictable and should be expected. Those who are building a Peer Coaching program must understand that even negative responses can play a positive role in facilitating the change process. Hence, perseverance is an important attribute of implementation. Members of the school community must also realize that "building trust is a complex venture that takes time, focus, nurturing, and energy. When it becomes a consistent characteristic of the workplace, however, there is no end to its positive influence" (Robbins & Alvy, 2014, p. 101).

Summary

Peer Coaching consists of two forms: *collaborative work* and *formal coaching*. Collaborative work engages professional colleagues in activities not related to a classroom observation, yet are focused on classroom practices that have the potential to positively affect student learning. Often such work provides opportunities for meaningful collaboration while trust among professional colleagues is developing, and it may support welcome engagement of peers when shortages of time or resources—financial and human—preclude classroom observations. Collaborative work can be integrated with existing structures such as PLCs. It can build the capacity of staff to address challenging initiatives as well as to promote the transfer of training and the refining of teacher practices and student learning. Formal coaching activities take place within the classroom context. They can include coteaching, but more often are framed around a structure that engages a coach and an inviting teacher in a pre-conference, a classroom observation of the teacher and students, and a post-conference. Ideally, both collaborative work and formal coaching should be voluntary. The goals of Peer Coaching should include becoming more reflective about instructional practices; learning about teaching strategies; deepening understanding of curriculum and assessment; and studying what enhances students' learning experiences in ways that culminate in their success. Just as the teacher learns as a consequence of being coached, another goal of the Peer Coaching process is that both parties learn about coaching strategies and how they affect thinking, behavior, and results.

Various factors may positively or negatively impact the Peer Coaching process, including organizational climate and culture, and the history of working relationships among professional colleagues. Most importantly, trust is the foundational underpinning for coaching. In particular, the principal's support for Peer Coaching has a decided effect on how coaching is perceived and whether or not it thrives. Chapter 3 discusses the foundation for collegial dialogue using structures for collaborative work.

Reflective Questions

1. Given the discussion of collaborative work and formal coaching, which type of activity do you believe would be most valuable in the context in which you work?

2. What types of coaching roles are currently in place at your school? Which are working well, and why? Which are experiencing challenges, and why?

3. How would you assess relational trust among professional colleagues in your school? Is there sufficient trust to provide the foundational underpinnings for coaching? Why or why not?

4. Given the overview of factors that positively or negatively influence the Peer Coaching process, how would you assess the context of your school? What will support or hinder Peer Coaching efforts?

3

....

Building a Foundation for Collegial Dialogue: Structures for Collaborative Work

When I think back to those days when I first started out, you had your interview with the principal, and off you went to your classroom. You were left there to come up with your ideas while master teachers went on doing what they did, and you never had time to reflect with anyone. You may have pondered why that lesson went well, or why it did not, never really having that extra set of eyes or ears to explore your speculations. Collaborative work structures create access to a library of expertise residing in classrooms just down the hall from mine. No longer am I alone.

—Veteran teacher, New York City

Examining the roots of the teaching profession can help us understand the challenges related to cultivating an environment that will nurture dialogue about teaching and learning—and the importance of creating such an environment. Teaching is rooted in a tradition of isolation. From the original one-room schoolhouse to the current structures of most schools, once described by Carl Glickman as the "one-room schoolhouse repeated every few yards down the corridor," (1990, pp. 68–72) the physical characteristics of schools and the norms of isolation—going it alone—impose barriers to communication about successful instructional, curricular, and assessment practices. As a result, many well-kept secrets exist in individual classrooms, and year after year, teachers leave their mark on students' learning experiences but not a trace on the teaching profession. Despite hundreds of years of collective staff experience in individual schools, few avenues exist for teachers to tap into this expertise. Fortunately, this workplace reality has begun to change in many schools.

In many settings, teachers and administrators have gone to extraordinary lengths to ensure that collegial work develops and prospers, giving voice to the wisdom of teachers in individual classrooms and adding to the collective knowledge base of staff and to the school's capacity to boost student learning. These schools have a shared belief that student success hinges on the teacher in the classroom, and that high-quality learning experiences designed by that teacher are the single best predictor of student success and achievement. Members of these school communities have articulated that belief by creating a vision of excellence focused on refining teaching practices to increase the resources available to promote student learning. A genuine commitment to this vision is evident in the careful planning that has structured time, financial resources, personnel, and professional development to support collegial dialogue that leads to teacher and student learning.

Peer Coaching Structures: Unleashing Staff Potential

Peer Coaching structures for collaborative work and formal coaching, as well as related collegial activities such as team meetings, create the medium that unleashes staff potential. Regardless of the form of coaching, its structures and activities lead to outcomes such as these:

• The creation of collaborative, learning-focused cultures that deepen skills in reflection, critical and creative thinking, problem solving, and the use of technology.

• The development of knowledge, skills, and refined teaching practices that lead to enhanced teacher quality, instructional decision making, and performance.

• Increased camaraderie and teacher satisfaction with workplace conditions.

• Resources focused on developing ideas and solutions to problems of practice and strategies to address evolving challenges and initiatives.

• Enhanced avenues to boost student achievement in strategic, data-driven ways.

• Opportunities that empower staff members to grow professionally through job-embedded learning opportunities and the learning-focused use of time.

The next sections describe the collaborative work structures and activities (listed in the first column of Figure 2.1, p. 24) that contribute to accomplishing these ends. (The structures related to formal coaching are described in Chapter 4.)

Storytelling About Teaching Practices

Creating narratives about teaching practices or even classroom dilemmas allows a teacher to share experiences with a colleague, but in a way that is one step removed from a formal coaching observation. A high school geometry teacher addressing the Common Core State Standard "Expressing geometric properties with equations" watched a YouTube video from math expert and former teacher Dan Meyer in which Meyer used the example of "shooting hoops" with a basketball to introduce the concept of a parabola (http://www.youtube.com/watch?v=jRMVjHjYB6w). After viewing the video, the geometry teacher went to work planning how she could use the basketball example with students in her classroom. The results were amazing. Students were highly engaged in predicting which basketball shots would go through the hoop and which would miss it. Following this, the teacher introduced the concept of a parabola, and because its image was grounded in the experience of watching the basketball video, the equation for the parabola and related vocabulary terms made sense to the students. They completed written problems with no errors! Excited about these results, the teacher texted a department colleague during her break and arranged to meet with her during their common planning time to share this experience. Sharing stories of successful practice deepened the teachers' conceptual understanding of curriculum concepts and expanded the resources available to them, contributing to the ongoing progress of students.

Video Analysis

As teachers implement curriculum or plan how they will address Common Core or state standards and benchmarks, they often wonder, What instructional approaches could I use to address this standard? Is there something I could add to my instructional repertoire? Several online resources provide answers to these questions. One such website is www.teachingchannel.org. Teachers can view and analyze videos on their own or with professional colleagues. For instance, a team of English language arts teachers met during a designated professional development time at their school. They had all been addressing poetic language and, more specifically, meaning in poetic language in several of their classes. Embedded in their lessons were Common Core standards such as "Use textual evidence to support ideas," "Analyze and determine deeper meaning of words in text," and "Determine figurative and connotative meaning of words in text." In addition to addressing these standards, the teachers were seeking ideas about how to increase students' active participation and to do so in a way that increased student responsibility for learning through the use of rubrics that reflected CCSS, such as "actively incorporate others in a discussion" and "summarize points of agreement." One of the teachers located a video on the Teaching Channel website in which a teacher used an instructional strategy called Socratic Seminar to address poetic language and a rubric to encourage students to reflect on their thinking and behavior. As the team watched the video, they not only analyzed the instructional approach, but also focused on how the scoring of the rubric changed over time. For example, what was "proficient" at the beginning of the semester became "basic" halfway through the semester. This approach offered a new way of assessing student learning. After analyzing the video, several of the teachers decided to coplan lessons, incorporating both the Socratic Seminar approach and the use of the rubric aligned with CCSS. In this example, the use of video analysis expanded the teachers' instructional repertoires and added interest and vitality to the students' learning experiences.

Problem Solving to Enrich Professional Practice

Among the many problem-solving models available, peer coaches often use one called Consulting Colleagues. Peers bring problems that they wish to solve to a meeting. First, they form groups of three and designate one person as "A," one as "B," and the third as "C." During Round 1, which lasts for five minutes, A shares a problem while B and C listen and take notes. During the next five minutes, B and C ask clarifying questions about the problem and A answers. Finally, during the last five minutes, B and C offer solution ideas to A, who records them. Notice that in this structure, the participants spend two-thirds of the time seeking to understand the problem before generating solution strategies. The process is repeated so that B and C have an opportunity to discuss their problems as well. Hence, in a 45-minute session, each teacher can address her own problem and serve as a resource to two colleagues. The Consulting Colleague interactions raise awareness among teachers that others encounter instructional dilemmas and build a shared realization that "if only I reach out, the answer to the problem I am grappling with exists just a few yards down the hallway!" The structure develops trust and interdependence among professional colleagues.

One elementary grade-level team used the Consulting Colleagues structure to address classroom challenges related to students with special needs, English language learners, and struggling students. After each person in the trio had a chance to share and glean resources from colleagues, a teacher offered this reflection: "Using the Consulting Colleagues model afforded me fresh perspectives on the problems I have struggled with and new ideas and resources to address these problems. I have a growing sense of respect for my colleagues and the tremendous resources that their colleagueship generates!"

Study Groups

Study groups can bring together small cohorts of teachers to focus on a topic of mutual interest or can involve an entire faculty in the collaborative study of a topic that is tied to site-based school improvement initiatives. Study groups can be formal or informal in nature, and the topics they address can range from the study of particular instructional approaches, such as differentiated instruction, to learning about working with children of poverty or homeless students. Study groups are a form of professional learning grounded in promoting professional conversations, collegial work, and learning about issues that directly affect teaching and learning. Whole-faculty study groups purposefully focus on "mobilizing" a faculty to examine a schoolwide issue related to a specific school improvement goal (Lick & Murphy, 2007). As a collaborative work structure, they offer teachers a sense of belonging and support as part of a group of colleagues focused on a particular challenge they face in classroom practice. A study group can involve its members in activities such as reading and discussing articles or books, doing Internet research, or conducting action research related to the chosen topic. They can be led by a specific teacher or teachers can rotate and share the role of facilitator. Staff members can engage face-to-face or include practitioners across schools in online chats. Ideally, study groups should meet regularly in 60- or 90-minute blocks of time, sufficient to allow "teachers to reflect, analyze, and critique practices together" (Saavedra, 1996, p. 273).

One group of middle school teachers in Chattanooga, Tennessee, decided to form a cross-discipline study group to learn about teaching students from poverty. The impetus for this focus came when the attendance boundaries for the school shifted and a large population from "the projects" became a part of the student body. The group selected *Turning High-Poverty Schools into High-Performing Schools* (Parrett & Budge, 2012) to read, and they discussed its implications for teaching and learning in their classrooms. Teachers reported that their study group activities generated an enhanced understanding of students from poverty and a better sense of what kinds of classroom and school experiences were needed to help this segment of the school community thrive. Their work led to networking electronically with other school staffs across the district that had worked with similar student populations, and generated the exchange of lesson plans and activities, as well as an online dialogue about expectations for homework.

Conversations About Student Work

Conversations about student work provide opportunities for faculty members to reflect on the results of lessons they have individually or collaboratively taught by examining artifacts of student work. This process builds capacity to respond to all students. Consultant Ann Delehant cites the following reasons for looking at student work:

- Identify strengths and shortcomings of the work.
- Diagnose, identify, or monitor student needs.
- Align curriculum, instruction, and assessment with student needs.
- Ensure that all students have equal access and opportunity to succeed.
- Guide curriculum development and refinement (related to Common Core).
- Improve teaching.
- Assess the merits of programs/initiatives.
- Assess the extent to which standards are addressed.
- Determine how students' work compares to outside norms.
(Personal communication, August 15, 2014)

Several protocols for conversations about student work exist. The example that follows was inspired by the work of Ann Delehant. Conversations about student work usually involve an inviting teacher (the individual who has asked colleagues to participate in the conversation about student work), a teacher facilitator for the conversation, and group members who are usually teacher colleagues, but might also be content area specialists or other individuals who have insights about the student(s) or the work.

Before the Conversation About Student Work. The inviting teacher collects artifacts for colleagues to examine during the session, based on the desired focus for the conversation. These may include the lesson plan, a description and examples of the assignment(s), rubrics for the assignment(s), and either a range of student work (high-medium-low performers) or an individual student's work that resulted from the assignment.

The Basics of a Student Work Conversation.

• The facilitator welcomes group members and explains the protocol that will be used during the conversation about student work. This may entail an overview of the steps of the process, the time allocation for each step, and the roles group members play.

• The inviting teacher describes the context for the student work. For example, what led up to the assignment; what might follow; or characteristics of the students. Group members review the assignment and the scoring rubric.

• The inviting teacher identifies a focusing question which serves to guide group members' dialogue and highlights the type of information that the inviting teacher wishes to examine. Group members may ask clarifying questions about the context, the rubric, or the focusing question, to which the inviting teacher provides answers.

• The inviting teacher then shares and reviews samples of student work. These can be original or copied works and sometimes might include video segments. For example, a teacher might bring a collection of writing samples that are passed among group members.

• Group members revisit the focusing question and then silently review the student work, making notes about what they would like to share during the feedback session.

• After student work has been examined, group members offer feedback while the inviting teacher is silent. Often the inviting teacher takes notes during this feedback session.

• The facilitator then asks the inviting teacher to respond to the feedback generated by group members. The inviting teacher may choose to address specific comments and questions which have the most meaning for him or her. During this segment of the conversation about student work, the facilitator may ask clarifying questions.

• Collectively, group members and the inviting teacher develop an action plan.

• The facilitator leads the group in reflecting upon the conversation experience. This may include questions about the universal applicability of the experience for the work of others, which questions or responses generated useful data, and what new questions have emerged.

Using this process gives the inviting teacher an opportunity to examine her practices and the resulting visible learning it produced, as evidenced by student work. It also affords all teachers in the group an opportunity to analyze teaching strategies, curriculum content, assessments, and student work. Additionally, the teachers are able to examine the implications for informing their collective practices. The learning-focused dialogue this experience produces builds trust among professional colleagues, a valuing of the perspectives of others, and a deeper understanding of the craft of teaching.

Book Talks

Book talks can involve small groups of teachers focused on a common topic of professional interest, or an entire faculty may choose to read a book that addresses a school improvement goal or a grade-level or subject-area focus of interest. The outcome of a book talk should be high-quality conversations that inspire critical thinking and reflection that ultimately affects teaching practices and student learning.

In one Northern California high school, math department teachers formed a book-talk group with the goal of learning more about the flipped classroom and how the concept could enhance the engagement of students in the math curriculum, as well as student performance. The teachers researched a variety of books and articles on the topic. Ultimately, each teacher selected a book or a collection of articles to read. They also attended a flipped classroom webinar together. After reading the books and articles and attending the webinar, they discussed highlights of the content. Then their conversations involved department members in deciding how their collective learnings would influence the practices in the math department. After implementing flipped-classroom practices for a semester, they examined the student work and feedback that was generated. They noted increased student mastery of mathematical concepts and a sense of eagerness among students to get the next assignment. Involvement in the book talk augmented the teachers' repertoires of strategies to address the math curriculum, increasing students' time on task and their enthusiasm for math classes.

Data Talks

> Teachers, administrators, and support staff need specific tools to generate meaningful data, illuminate relationships between instructional interventions and student performance data, and facilitate conversations so that appropriate and responsive interventions can be designed, implemented, and carefully monitored with the end result being high levels of student learning. (Hess & Robbins, 2012, pp. xi–xii)

Data Talks engage teachers in meaningful conversations about data by providing specific structures that enable them to do the following:

- Reflect upon and carefully examine data.
- Ask meaningful questions about data to clarify and identify problems.
- Determine possible reasons for problems in student performance.
- Conduct action planning.
- Implement action plans.
- Collect data.
- Evaluate results.

Teachers on a 6th grade team in Minnesota used a Data Talks strategy called Three Guiding Questions to think through the most important knowledge and skills they wanted students to learn in their language arts classrooms. With this information, they thought through how they would assess the critical knowledge and skills identified and what they needed to do to provide intervention or extension activities for students in need of additional support. Though this strategy was used by a team, it could also be used by individuals to address a particular standard that students are not reaching based upon assessment data. Teachers may also use this strategy when designing instruction to address outcomes that will be assessed, either locally or on a state assessment. Here are the Three Guiding Questions:

> Question 1: What critical knowledge and/or skills (learning targets) does each student need to have or be able to perform during this unit/course of study? (This can also be state or national content standards.)

> Question 2: How will we know when each student has learned it? Assessments can be informal, such as checking for understanding, or formal and should be meaningful to the student and measure the learning target being assessed. Common assessments, agreed upon assessment tools, and rubrics facilitate conversations about student performance and lead to instructional improvement and student learning.

> Question 3: How will we respond when a student needs intervention or extension along the way so that each student meets (or exceeds) the learning target? This question involves progress monitoring and interventions. (Hess & Robbins, 2012, pp. 26–29)

The three guiding questions support professional colleagues in thinking through how they assess critical knowledge and skills, and what they can do to provide intervention or extension activities.

As staff members engage in data talks, their collective capacity to design systems to collect data, analyze data, develop and implement interventions, and produce desired results increases dramatically. Relationships among professional colleagues are strengthened, trust increases, and achievement flourishes.

Coplanning Lessons

Coplanning lessons is another collaborative work structure that leads to refinement in teaching practices, articulated curriculum, and student learning. Many lesson-planning templates are available; hence, as colleagues meet to coplan lessons, they should first dialogue about the lesson-planning models they use and select one that is mutually agreeable. Figure 3.1 is an example of a template that teachers have used in their collaborative work. In many instances after teachers coplan lessons, they individually teach the lessons in their classrooms and collect samples of student work. Then they meet, compare the student work generated by the lesson, and dialogue about how they might tweak the lesson. In other cases, if trust is present and schedules permit, the teachers may coteach the lesson.

Many teachers use coplanning to produce interdisciplinary lessons. One pair of teachers developed an integrated English and social studies lesson. Another pair created an integrated math and science lesson. After coplanning three lessons with a colleague, a teacher offered the following reflection:

> Working together with a colleague enabled me to witness how another person thinks about organizing for instruction, presenting content, planning for student engagement, and assessing learning. My resources have expanded and the quality of the lesson and student work is enhanced.

Many Possibilities, Many Benefits

Collaborative work can take numerous forms, limited only by the imaginations and creativity of those who participate. The structures described in this chapter are but a few examples. The ones that teachers use should reflect the professional learning goals they set for themselves, their interests, local initiatives, and student performance. Whenever possible, it is useful to integrate collaborative work with existing collegial structures such as PLC meetings, faculty forums, grade-level

FIGURE 3.1

Template for Collaborative Lesson Planning

Opening Activity (focus task, pre-assessment, overview, purpose, outcomes):

Instruction, Modeling, Checking for Understanding:

High-Quality Engagement (rubrics/success criteria for work, graphic organizers, comparison tasks, interaction strategies, summarizing, note taking):

Guided Practice (with teacher monitoring; making midcourse corrections; providing feedback; remediation):

Critical Thinking Skills (which thinking skills are involved and how will students demonstrate these?):

Social-Emotional Learning (personal relevance, acceptance of diversity, sense of belonging, empathy, collaboration structures, handling relationships):

Closing Activities (tasks provided so that students can reflect upon and summarize the lesson and assess their own performance):

Independent Practice (independent work within the classroom or homework):

Additional Topics for discussion (e.g., use of technology; student work to be assigned):

or department meetings, or subject-area data-team meetings so that it becomes an integrated, viable, and functional part of the culture.

Participation in collaborative work develops trust among professional colleagues over time as teachers engage with one another, share challenges, and find solutions. Professionals have an opportunity to refine their thinking about planning and teaching practices, teachers enhance their skillfulness, students' learning experiences are infused with greater quality, and achievement soars. Collaborative work activities and structures aid in developing a comfort level around working with trusted colleagues, and they intensify the strategic focus on teaching and learning in the workplace. These outcomes provide the essential foundation for formal coaching.

Summary

Collaborative work strategies can take many forms. Among these are storytelling about teaching practices, video analysis, problem solving, study groups, conversations about student work, book talks, data talks, and coplanning lessons. In all of these structures, as teachers work together, trust develops and they have the opportunity to practice critical thinking skills. Teachers learn how their colleagues conceptualize the curriculum, make plans to teach it, design student work, teach, assess student learning, monitor learning and adjust teaching strategies, integrate technology, and build relationships among students. Collectively, these job-embedded learning experiences provide the essential foundation for formal coaching. Chapter 4 will provide an overview of the formal coaching process.

Reflective Questions

1. As you ponder the rationale for collaborative work activities and think of the unique characteristics of the culture in which you work, which collaborative approaches do you believe would best fit workplace norms? Which would represent a "stretch"? Which activities would fit well with existing collaborative structures such as PLCs?

2. After reading this chapter, which of the structures would have the greatest impact for laying the foundation for formal coaching in your school? Why?

3. In addition to the eight collaborative work examples presented in this chapter, in what other ways might teachers collaborate to refine teaching practices and enhance student learning (e.g., collaborate to develop common assessments or to articulate the curriculum)?

4. Suppose staff members wanted to study brain research and its implications for teaching and learning. Which strategies would you use to collaboratively engage colleagues so that their work would result in brain-compatible teaching approaches that enhanced student learning?

4

....

Investigating the Components of Formal Coaching

Teaching is so isolated. It's so valuable to continue to learn.

—Kelly Gary, 1st Grade Teacher
Lower School, Sewickley Academy

Formal coaching builds upon a foundation of collaborative work, discussed in Chapter 3, to continue to break through the isolation that can permeate the teaching profession. It provides an opportunity for teachers to learn about their practices and the consequences of those practices. Formal, in-classroom Peer Coaching involves teacher colleagues working together with a focus on the observation of teaching. Formal coaching is a job-embedded form of professional learning intended to enhance professional practice in ways that shape and enhance both the teaching profession and student learning. Formal coaching can involve two teachers coteaching a lesson, then reflecting on what happened as they expected and what happened differently, and analyzing their professional learning and the learning of students. Although formal coaching can include coteaching, most often it involves a teacher known as the *inviting teacher* who invites a *coach*, usually a teacher colleague, to engage in a pre-conference, an observation with a focus determined by the inviting teacher, and a post-conference.

Garmston (1987) helpfully identified and defined three different forms of coaching: technical, collegial, and challenge. *Technical coaching* focuses on the learning and transfer of new skills and strategies into teachers' existing repertoires. *Collegial coaching* focuses on the context of teaching and the need for self-reflection and professional dialogue among teachers to improve practice and positively affect the orga-nizational context to support that improvement. *Challenge coaching* addresses specific and persistent problems in instructional design and delivery that need attention. The "formal coaching" to which this book is dedicated focuses on what Garmston refers to as "collegial coach-ing." To put things in a broader context, however, it should be noted that since Garmston's 1987 article was published, various other types of coaching have emerged, in both business and education. Zepeda (2012) notes several of these, including executive coaching (Goldsmith, Lyons, & Freas, 2000); cognitive coaching (Costa & Garmston, 2002); differentiated coaching (Kise, 2006); literacy coaching (Casey, 2006; Dozier, 2006); math coaching (Kenney, Hancewicz, Heuer, Metsisto, & Tuttle, 2005); instructional coaching (Knight, 2007); and mentor coaching (Nolan, 2007).

Intended Outcomes

The intended outcomes of the formal coaching process for the inviting teacher are the development of reflective practice and decision making; a refined and expanded repertoire of teaching strategies; an enhanced understanding of instruction, curriculum, and assessment; and the capacity to provide enriched learning environments for students char-acterized by interesting and engaging work. The result? High-quality teaching that generates improved student learning.

For the teacher functioning as coach, the intended outcomes are an enhanced capacity to build rapport with the inviting teacher so that meaningful and productive coaching conversations and observations can take place. Additionally, the coach develops an increased under-standing of questioning strategies that invite a teacher to reflect upon the planning that preceded a lesson, the lesson context, and one's teaching practices and their consequences. Ultimately, the coach's questions have the potential to increase the teacher's awareness of student performance and related midcourse corrections. The coach's questions also help the teacher to analyze and refine instructional strategies that produce desired results, and to plan instructional next steps. Ideally, the coach also learns which coaching practices inhibit thinking and action planning and how to transform those practices so that difficult conversations are possible and result in refined coaching strategies, increased teacher skillfulness, and improved student learning.

An Overview of Formal Coaching

The most common type of formal coaching is a traditional structured approach that includes a pre-conference, an observation, and a post-conference. The following sections briefly describe each of these components. (Chapters 5, 6, and 7 provide additional, in-depth examinations of each.)

The Pre-Conference

The pre-conference precedes the observation. The late Madeline Hunter once told a group of coaching participants why it is so important:

> A good pre-conference is worth several post-conferences, because the pre-conference provides the teacher with an opportunity to "rehearse" the lesson before it actually takes place, while building the coach's understanding of that lesson. It is in this context that the coach learns what the teacher desires the coach to focus upon during the observation, what that professional is genuinely curious about, and how the teacher thinks about teaching and learning.

Hence the pre-conference is an essential part of the formal coaching process.

At the pre-conference, the coach asks the inviting teacher to explain the purpose of the lesson, the instructional strategies to be used, what led up to the lesson and what will follow, how students will be engaged, and indicators of success. The coach might also ask about student characteristics and class norms for behavior, as well as any concerns about the lesson or observation. The inviting teacher explains the lesson to be taught and specifics regarding the focus of the observation. Together, the coach and the inviting teacher decide how the data might best be collected. Generally, the focus is something the teacher is genuinely curious about; it might have an instructional, curricular, or student emphasis. Essentially, it is as if the teacher is a researcher in his own classroom, and the coach is the data collector. The discussion between colleagues usually includes talk about where the coach should sit or stand to collect data and whether the coach should interact with students. The inviting teacher also determines the parameters for the discussion of the lesson at the post-conference.

The coach's role during the pre-conference is to facilitate the inviting teacher's thinking about and planning for the lesson—to afford a "dress rehearsal" of the actual teaching performance. This role usually includes asking probing and clarifying questions that serve two purposes. First, they help the teacher to fine-tune thinking about the lesson and desired student outcomes, and, at times, to develop a fallback plan in case the lesson doesn't go as envisioned. Second, these questions assist the coach by clarifying the desired focus of the observation and by specifying how the data are to be collected. The pre-conference generally concludes with the coach asking for feedback about what she did during the pre-conference to facilitate the teacher's thinking before the lesson, and what the inviting teacher wished the coach might have done differently. This feedback allows the coach to reflect and determine which coaching strategies are helpful so that these can be repeated in future sessions. Asking for feedback in this way also models a spirit of reciprocity. The coach is committed to working just as seriously in the coaching role as the teacher is in the teaching role. This duality ultimately contributes to the establishment of a trusting relationship.

The Observation

The focus of the observation is determined by the inviting teacher. Examples of areas for focus include critical thinking skills, teacher-student interaction, student time on task, transitions, wait time, verbal flow, use of a particular instructional strategy and its effects, student engagement using technology, active participation, a specific student's behavior, or the effects of a curricular approach. The inviting teacher determines the focus so it reflects what has significance for that teacher and so the discussion of observed teaching in the post-conference reflects the desired focus.

In the early stages of a Peer Coaching relationship, the inviting teacher often picks a safe focus—one that is likely to yield positive data. As trust builds between the coach and the teacher and the two have the opportunity to switch roles, the inviting teacher might be more willing to experiment and take risks. As one teacher put it, as she grew more comfortable with the Peer Coaching process, she realized that "anything worth doing is worth doing poorly at first!"

Coaching should be a dynamic process. The focus of observations will change as the inviting teacher wishes. For instance, on one occasion an inviting teacher asked her coach to observe during a unit on World War II in her social studies class, and she requested that the coach record the questions she asked, how many seconds she waited before eliciting student responses, which students responded, and what they said. When the inviting teacher examined the observation data with the coach, she expressed her surprise that during the lesson several students had questions about the Holocaust, and some had not heard of it. As the teacher and the coach discussed the student responses and the teacher's desire to include lessons about social and emotional learning as an integrated part of the social studies curriculum in future lessons, the two formulated a plan for the next lesson. It would address the Holocaust and embed lessons related to emotional intelligence. The coach also shared the e-mail address of a teacher friend in Virginia who was using the social studies curriculum as a backdrop for a unit on tolerance. The inviting teacher began an online conversation with the teacher in Virginia that provided additional resources for the lesson. During the next observation, the coach was asked to focus on evidence of social and emotional learning (with indicators specified by the inviting teacher). The inviting teacher asked the coach to use a video camera to record the lesson so that she could see both the verbal and nonverbal responses of students.

Before the observation, the inviting teacher usually tells the class about the coach's visit: "Ms. Gray will be coming in to watch me teach today. At another time, I will be visiting her classroom. At this school, teachers believe in learning from one another." Many teachers have commented that making statements such as these affords them an opportunity to model, at an adult level, the type of cooperative learning they are promoting in their own classrooms among students.

The Post-Conference

Post-conferences are diverse and can be categorized into three types: mirroring, collaborative, and expert (which includes an expert advisor, mentor, or resource provider). The type used depends on the preference of the inviting teacher and is often influenced by the time available to meet, the trust between the coach and the teacher, as well as the history of the coaching relationship.

The mirroring post-conference requires the least time and might be selected if the time available is short or if the teacher does not desire a lot of dialogue about the observation. In the mirroring post-conference, the coach simply says, "Here are the data you asked me to collect. If you have any questions, please let me know and we can schedule a time to discuss the data." The coach then hands the data from the observation over to the teacher. Data collection can include scripting, the use of teacher-designed instruments, or video recordings. The coach's role in this example is that of a confidential, objective observer and data collector. In this form of coaching, the inviting teacher analyzes the data alone.

In a collaborative conference, the conversation usually is characterized by a mutual discussion of the teaching observed. The coach asks the inviting teacher to reflect on what happened as expected or planned and what happened differently. The inviting teacher also analyzes what teaching and student behaviors contributed to the lesson outcomes.

After the inviting teacher has had an opportunity to reflect, the coach shares the observational data. Out of this discussion, the teacher determines what changes to make when teaching the lesson again. At the end of the conference, the coach solicits feedback about the coaching strategies employed. Throughout the post-conference, the discussion is guided by the parameters set forth by the inviting teacher in the pre-conference. The inviting teacher decides what to do with the data. Sometimes the coach helps plan the initial lesson in the pre-conference and, in the post-conference, collaboratively analyzes and helps replan the lesson if it is to be taught again. This type of post-conference might take as long as 30 to 50 minutes and involves a much deeper, mutual analysis of the data.

In an expert conference, the coach is an expert who has more experience or expertise in either a grade level or with a particular instructional, curricular, or assessment technique. In the post-conference, the expert guides the inviting teacher to analyze the lesson, much as the coach does in the collaborative conference. The expert conference differs from the collaborative one, however, in that the coach often teaches during the pre- and post-conference. For example, one novice teacher asked her coach to analyze the variety of ways that students were asked to actively participate in her lesson. The coach wrote down specific examples of active participation during the lesson observation. At the post-conference, the novice reflected, "I used 'think, pair, share,' choral responses, signaling, and clickers, but I wish I could have used additional strategies. Could you share some other approaches with me?" The coach responded with an inquiry: "What other techniques have you tried in previous lessons?" The novice recalled her use of response cards and individual whiteboards. In this example, the expert facilitated the novice's reflection and rehearsal of strategies used in the past. This questioning increased the likelihood that the teacher could recall the techniques quickly in the future. The expert's questioning facilitated the novice's recall of past efforts and provided a strategy that the novice could use in the future, even when the expert coach wasn't there. Thus the post-conference strengthened the teacher's ability to help herself—a vital survival skill in isolated classrooms. The coach provided additional strategies after the novice had the opportunity to reflect. If the novice had not been able to recall any techniques used in the past, the expert might have shared some of those she had seen others use and then asked the novice to consider which might best suit the particular lesson, her teaching style, and students. Even in the expert conference, the inviting teacher has control over what happens and how the data are used. The expert post-conference usually takes 30 minutes to an hour. Trust is a critical factor in the expert conference because some teachers fear that acknowledging an instructional difficulty or asking for assistance might be construed as an open admission of incompetence (Rosenholtz, 1989).

The mirroring, collaborative, and expert forms of the post-conference are not a developmental continuum. They represent a range of options for interaction between the inviting teacher and the coach. For example, the inviting teacher might work with an expert coach for one observation to learn more about teaching social skills in a cooperative-learning lesson using tablet computers. In the next coaching session, the inviting teacher might ask the same coach to collaboratively plan, observe, and discuss a lesson using social skills within a technology lesson. The third time they work together, the inviting teacher might ask the coach to function as a mirror and to observe student time on task in a cooperative-learning lesson in which students work in pairs with their tablets to conduct research. The collective goal of the coaching sessions is to facilitate the teacher's ability to reflect upon and analyze teaching and its influence on student learning. The teacher plays the role of action researcher in his own classroom. He is assisted by the coach, who serves as a data collector and, in some cases, as a co-investigator.

In contrast to the collegial Peer Coaching discussed in the previous paragraphs, in technical coaching, the pre- and post-conferencing is tied to a specific strategy or curricular approach taught during a professional session. Here, the purpose of coaching is to facilitate skill transfer from the workshop to the workplace. In this instance, the observation focus is not steered by the inviting teacher; it is linked to the workshop content. Hence if the workshop addresses the elements of a specific lesson strategy, such as Socratic Seminar, the coaching process revolves around the classroom implementation of this strategy or innovation.

Regardless of the form of the post-conference—mirror, collaborative, or expert—the coach *always* gives the data that were collected during the observation to the inviting teacher at the conclusion of the post-conference. The inviting teacher chooses how to use the data. Symbolically, this action of handing over the data communicates and emphasizes the nonevaluative nature of coaching.

Logistical Considerations

As noted in previous chapters, preparing the culture for Peer Coaching is essential in order that authentic, learning-focused communications can occur during formal coaching interactions. Providing a spectrum of collaborative work opportunities helps build a climate and a comfort level that sustain rich conversations about teaching and learning. This collaborative work breaks down walls between classrooms and builds a robust, abundant knowledge bank from which all teachers can draw. Although many schools and districts have instituted Peer Coaching to complement the implementation of a systemwide teacher accountability process—and, indeed, coaching practices can enhance and refine planning for, delivering, and assessing instruction—it is worth repeating, and emphasizing, that Peer Coaching *should not be connected to supervision or evaluation in any way.* "Supervision is incompatible with healthy coaching relations. The presence of evaluation prejudices the necessary willingness to show weakness and vulnerability in order to gain support" (Hargreaves & Dawe, 1990, p. 238). When coaching is mandated, it runs the risk of becoming what Hargreaves (1989, 1994) has appropriately labeled "contrived collegiality," an activity that forces unwanted contacts among unconsenting adults, consuming already scarce time. Hargreaves and Dawe emphasize the following:

> We… very much support teachers improving their skills by work-
> ing closely and practically with each other, especially where that
> process is genuinely voluntary, where teachers have high con-
> trol over determining and reflecting about which skills are to
> be coached, and where critical reflection about the content and
> context of those skills is not only permitted but actively encour-
> aged…. [W]e recognize too that administrative leadership and
> facilitation (though not supervision and intrusive control) are
> almost certainly needed to further the development of these rela-
> tionships, which bring together practicality, collegiality, and criti-
> cal reflection in an innovatory mix. (p. 239)

The classic understanding afforded by Hargreaves and Dawe has
important implications for the design of the structures and activities of
both collaborative work and formal coaching.

How often Peer Coaching partners meet is a function of desire or
need, as well as opportunity, given budgets for release time or availability of substitutes. Many coaching partners overcome some of these con-
straints by meeting electronically before and after an observation, or
they use video cameras or Videre (an iPad observation app, described
in Chapter 1) to capture teaching episodes, after which the data are
shared. Peer Coaching partners often meet twice a month so that each
individual can play the role of inviting teacher as well as coach. Time
for coaching comes from a variety of sources: released time associated
with school improvement programs, prep periods, and substitute
teachers. In some settings, teachers form trios. Teacher A assumes
responsibility for her class and teacher B's, which frees B to observe
C. In other contexts, specialists work with classes to free a teacher
to coach, or a principal or an assistant principal will teach a class to
release a teacher for coaching. An elementary teacher in a school that
used substitute teachers to support Peer Coaching offered this advice:

> We referred to our substitutes as "guest teachers" to enhance their
> status in the eyes of students. And we provided them with spe-
> cialized training in classroom management. We requested the
> same subs all year long to afford a measure of continuity. We

also communicated to parents about what we were doing. We focused on measures that minimized the loss of our student contact time and maximized the gains generated by our Peer Coaching involvement.

Time is a critical ingredient for successful Peer Coaching. For Peer Coaching activities to be purposeful and productive, adequate time should be allocated for the pre-conference, the observation, and the post-conference. Time allocated for the pre-conference should be sufficient so that the inviting teacher can reflect upon the lesson to be taught, share the planning process, identify the observation focus and the data-collection method, and discuss any other details pertinent to the observation. The time set aside for the observation must be appropriate to the observation task. For instance, if the inviting teacher wants the coach to focus on opening and closing activities and evidence of student learning, the coach needs to be present for the entire class period. The post-conference requires time for both the teacher and the coach to reflect upon the lesson, to converse about the observation focus and the data collected, and to generate instructional next steps and feedback about the coaching process.

Time for coaching should be scheduled so that it does not conflict with significant events in the classroom or the school (e.g., the end of a grading period, testing, open house) and so that it facilitates purposeful pairing for in-classroom observations. Coaching participants have indicated the need to have input into the scheduling to facilitate coaching between teachers at the same grade level or contiguous grade levels, teachers of the same subject areas, or teachers who have common professional interests, such as literacy approaches for English language learners.

Peer Coaching should occur in a psychologically and emotionally safe environment. To that end, teachers should choose their coaching partners. This selection is often based on shared interests or challenges, areas of expertise, friendship patterns, geographic proximity in the building, common schedules, similar teaching styles, a desire to expand their style, or the grade level or subject area that they teach. Some teachers purposefully choose coaching partners who have a style similar to theirs; others desire to work with a partner who has a different style. In one school, an entire grade-level team of four teachers worked together. Collectively, they coplanned a lesson. Then they pre-conferenced with one teacher on the team who volunteered to teach the lesson in each team member's classroom as the teacher from that classroom observed and collected data. Finally, the entire team post-conferenced together and decided how they would modify the lesson if it were to be taught again.

Coaching relationships that don't serve each party well should be terminated. As one teacher recommends, "You should have a rule that peer coaches can get a divorce if the relationship is not working!" Peer coaches in some schools change every semester. In other schools they remain constant. Who works with whom and for how long should reflect teacher choice. Every teacher should have the opportunity to play the roles of both inviting teacher and coach. The stance for the coach should be "I agree to work just as hard in the coaching role as the teacher does in the teaching role."

The care with which Peer Coaching relationships are established and nurtured over time is important and can be accomplished in a variety of ways. One school used personality styles as a tool to begin talking about participants' preferences, similarities, and differences. They examined how style influenced their own instructional decisions and how often it served as the lens through which they watched colleagues practice their craft. They also spoke of the moral obligation they all had to serve students with a multitude of personality styles in their classrooms. "This approach sensitized me to how my own predispositions could tempt me to judge others. As a result of this self-awareness, I believe I am now a more objective coach. It was a powerful experience," one teacher reflected.

Educators who want to incorporate styles into Peer Coaching can tap into several resources. Silver and Hanson (1996) invite educators to consider style from three perspectives: self, teaching style, and students' learning styles. Faculties in many schools have found this resource transformative in how they plan, deliver, and assess instruction. After learning about style, one high school math teacher in Henry County, Virginia, exclaimed, "This session on style made me aware that I was teaching to one quarter of my class—the fourth who learned like I did!" Hence, focusing on style with staff members not only has the potential to positively affect coaching relationships by developing an understanding of self and others; it also affects classroom practices as teachers discover how style influences lessons, the student work they design, and, consequently, student learning.

Several schools have studied the work of Harvard business professor Bill George and his book *True North* in their efforts to create a strong foundation for coaching relationships. George (2007) states, "True North is the internal compass that guides you successfully through life. It represents who you are as a human being at your deepest level. It is your orienting point—your fixed point in a spinning world—that helps you stay on track as a leader" (p. xxiii). Each coaching partner explores his or her "True North" and responds in writing to the prompt "What guides you successfully through life?" Conversations among coaching partners after these writing tasks engage professional colleagues in reflecting on the concept of True North and how core values influence and guide their behavior. This activity is often one that coaching partners come back to when they experience discord or differences in perception; it facilitates difficult conversations that often stem from such differences.

In some settings, teachers have developed questionnaires that coaching partners respond to in order to enhance understanding, build trust, create rapport, and develop a sturdy foundation for their coaching work. The form often includes questions such as these:

- What led you to enter the teaching profession?
- As a teacher, what are your core values?
- What are your beliefs about student learning?
- What drives you as a teacher?
- What pushes your buttons?

- What do you desire/value in a coach?
- How do you prefer to receive feedback? Give feedback?
- What are your professional growth goals?
- What are your strengths?
- What challenges you?
- Anything else you'd like to share?

Taking time to create an understanding of one another develops a sense of value for another's perspective and facilitates authentic communication, including building the foundation for difficult conversations among coaching partners. When it is clear to both parties that the intent is not to harm, but rather to grow professionally, those positive intentions will make difficult conversations possible and much more productive.

In schools that have laid the groundwork for Peer Coaching—cultivating the climate and culture of the organization and relationships among professional colleagues—Peer Coaching practices flourish, teaching performance is enhanced, and student learning thrives. Building a foundation and adhering to agreed-upon coaching practices are key to this results-oriented approach.

Summary

Formal coaching may consist of two teachers coteaching, or it may be a process in which an *inviting teacher* invites a *coach* to engage in a pre-conference, a classroom observation, and a post-conference. Both individuals have intended outcomes related to functioning in their respective roles, and each is expected to contribute to the success of the partnership. During the pre-conference the coach gathers information from the inviting teacher about the lesson to be observed, and the inviting teacher states what the focus of the observation should be. Together they determine how data will be collected. During the observation, the coach gathers the relevant data. Post-conferences can be categorized into three types: *mirroring, collaborative,* and *expert.* In all three, it is important to emphasize that *coaching is separate from evaluation.*

Building a supportive culture is an essential prerequisite for formal coaching. Cultural considerations include providing sufficient time for teachers to engage in the process and ensuring that they feel emotionally and psychologically safe in doing so. Developing true collaboration, as opposed to "contrived collegiality," requires understanding, rapport, and trust among Peer Coaching partners as well as leadership support. Trust, understanding, and rapport lead to meaningful conversations and strategic actions that culminate in refined teaching practices and student learning. Chapter 5 explores the pre-conference in greater detail.

Reflective Questions

1. What new insights do you have about formal coaching as a result of reading this chapter?

2. What logistical issues regarding Peer Coaching will present themselves at the school where you work? How might you address these?

3. Tom Bird and Judith Warren Little (1986) write, "Satisfying the requirement of reciprocity is the difference between meddling and support, between management and leadership" (p. 502). What do you think they mean by this?

4. Which of the approaches or strategies for cultivating a relationship between coaching partners resonated with you? What else might you suggest to build understanding and rapport so that results-oriented actions can follow?

5

Creating the Effective
Pre-Conference

*It is important to work out expectations in the pre-conference first so that you
are all on the same page when it comes to the observation and post-conference.*
—A 20-year veteran high school history teacher in Chicago

Perhaps the most essential and yet fragile component of formal coaching is the conferencing process, which entails a pre-conference before an observation and a post-conference following that observation. The success of conferencing is deeply rooted in the relationship that has been established between the coach and the inviting teacher, as well as the technical finesse the coach demonstrates in asking questions and using silence to facilitate the teacher's thinking. Taking time to build a trusting relationship yields the rapport necessary to create the space for an engaging conversation about teaching and learning. Without it, fear lurks. Individuals feel vulnerable and uncomfortable about exposing thoughts and classroom challenges.

Goleman, Boyatzis, and McKee (2002) explain: "Great leadership works through the emotions." Coaches who model emotionally intelligent leadership "have found effective ways to understand and improve the way they handle their own and other people's emotions" (pp. 3–5). They are able to read emotions in others by observing facial expressions and body language, and they use this information in determining how to respond, in terms of both words and tone. This ability brings comfort and enables the inviting teacher to express thoughts without hesitation. The technical aspect of conferencing involves the coach's understanding of how to develop and pose questions that foster reflection, analysis, and critical and creative thinking that will lead to refinements and insights about teaching practices and their consequences. Listening adds an important and vital dimension to the coach's work. Together, the coach's questions and listening skills create the avenues a teacher needs to express thoughts about planning, delivering, and assessing a lesson, and the student performance generated as a consequence of these collective efforts. Through the coaching process, the inviting teacher gains a new perspective of her classroom.

The Stance for Conferencing

Being observed by a peer is a new experience for some teachers. In addition, functioning as a coach puts some teachers on unfamiliar ground, so they may approach the conferencing and observation process with apprehension. Supporting both the inviting teacher and the teacher functioning as coach requires offering a stance as well as skills about what to say and how to say it. Judith Warren Little (1985) describes a helpful stance from which the teacher and coach can approach the discussion of a teaching episode: "There needs to be a spirit of curiosity about teaching and learning," as if the teacher and coach are "unraveling a mystery together, not monitoring each other." It is essential that the coach look for and collect data about the teaching practice that the inviting teacher has designated as the focus for the observation. But this must be done in a way that does not put the inviting teacher's sense of competence or self-esteem at stake. Asking questions that invite the teacher to reflect on practice—instead of the coach making statements—will generate rich and meaningful conversations.

Six Principles for Effective Conferencing

Little (1985) describes six principles that help in "separating the practice of teaching from the person conducting the lesson." This allows the practice of teaching to be analyzed without an attack on an individual's competence. The principles are organized into two categories: technical and social.

Technical Principles

Common language. A common language is helpful to describe, understand, and refine teaching. If common language (often involving terms related to a program or an initiative) does not exist, the coach and teacher can ask one another specific questions to elicit clarity and understanding of the terminology each person uses, thus enhancing the quality of dialogue during conferencing. For instance, if the teacher uses the term "concept attainment" to describe a teaching strategy she plans to use and the coach is unfamiliar with the term, the coach might ask, "Could you explain the process of concept attainment? I'm not familiar with it." Often taking the time to clarify an unfamiliar term in common language makes the point clearer to the sender as well as the receiver of the information. This situation offers an opportunity for coaches to experience professional growth at the same time they are filling a role designed to generate professional learning for the teacher.

Focus. A specific focus is critical because it narrows the parameters of what is to be observed and discussed. Setting limits in this way can be a comfort for the inviting teacher because it clearly establishes what the focus of the observation will be and what the corresponding dialogue will be about. The absence of surprises eases the concerns of the teacher who is to be observed. For the coach, narrowing the focus makes the data collection more concrete and precise, allowing the notes or video taken during the observation to be tightly aligned with the focus the inviting teacher has specified.

Hard evidence. Peer Coaching partners use objective data that becomes the source from which questions stem, analysis occurs, and conclusions are drawn. Going back to the data gathered without interpretation during the observation ensures that the dialogue between teacher and coach throughout the post-conference is based on an objective record of evidence, not a subjective interpretation.

Social Principles

Interaction. Peer Coaching partners interact in both the pre-conference and the post-conference. In some cases, the coach and the teacher may even interact during the observation, depending on the agreements negotiated during the pre-conference or situations that arise during the observation. For example, a teacher may whisper to the coach, "While I'm working with the small group, would you observe how students are performing in the three groups that are working independently? Because of my group's responses, now I'm curious about whether the work I prescribed is at the correct level of difficulty. Having data about what students say, questions they raise, and comments they make will help me determine that." Conferencing serves as a vehicle for joint work that leads to high-quality teaching, learning, and well-developed conferencing skills, fueling the competencies of both teacher and coach.

Predictability. When expectations lead to actions consistent with those expectations, a measure of predictability exists. Predictability helps Peer Coaching partners build and maintain trust. For instance, when the coach collects data according to the focus specified by the inviting teacher, then discusses only what the teacher has requested be the focus and consistently honors the agreement of confidentiality, the inviting teacher comes to rely on this predictability. Over time, this predictability creates respect and perceptions of credibility, contributing to the comfort that sustains productive conversations.

Reciprocity. Peer Coaching partners "build trust by acknowledging and deferring to one another's knowledge and skill, by talking to each other in ways that preserve individual dignity, and by giving their work together a full measure of energy, thought, and attention" (Little, 1985). The coach vows to work just as hard at conferencing and observing in the coaching role as the teacher does in the teaching role.

The Goals of Conferencing: Learning from Cognitive Coaching

The conferencing approaches of formal coaching are informed by the classic Cognitive Coaching work of Costa and Garmston (2002). Attesting to the idea that teaching is one of the most cognitively complex of all professions, Costa (2010) asserts, "It is the invisible skills of teaching, the thinking processes that underlie instructional decisions, which produce superior instruction."

Cognitive Coaching is a process during which teachers explore the thinking behind their practices. It has three goals: *trust, learning,* and *autonomy.* "The ultimate goal of Cognitive Coaching is teacher autonomy: the ability to self-monitor, self-analyze, and self-evaluate" (Garmston, Linder, & Whitaker, 1993, p. 58). Initially, the coach, through reflective questioning, pausing, paraphrasing, and pressing for specificity elicits the teacher's capacities in these areas. However, with time and practice, the teacher develops the internal capacity and expertise to plan, reflect, problem solve, and make decisions that ultimately enhance the quality of learning experiences in which students engage and from which they benefit. The focus in coaching is on the cognitive development of the person being coached. The "core belief is that a) everyone is capable of changing, b) teaching performance is based on decision-making skills that motivate skill development and refinement, and c) teachers are capable of enhancing each other's cognitive processes, decisions, and teaching behaviors" (Garmston, 1987, in Zepeda, 2012, p.149).

Cognitive Coaching cycles involve a pre-observation conference, a classroom observation, and a post-observation conference. Trust is the building block for the type of coaching relationship that enables both the coach and the inviting teacher to move beyond their current level of performance, grow professionally, and increase student achievement. Hence the individuals engaged in Peer Coaching must have trust in each other, trust in the coaching process, trust that all coaching interactions will remain confidential, and trust that Peer Coaching is not a remedial process but rather one that provides the opportunities for both the teacher and the coach to grow and learn from one another.

The Pre-Conference in Context

The pre-conference establishes the expectations and the parameters for the observation. The focus and guidelines for the observation are described during the pre-conference by the teacher who is to be observed. The pre-conference and the observation experience, during which the coach collects data, provide the reference points around which conversations will unfold during the post-conference.

How the Pre-Conference Works

During the pre-conference, the inviting teacher explains to the coach what the lesson to be observed will be about, what led up to the lesson, the expected teacher and student behaviors, the desired focus for the observation, how data are to be collected, details about the observation, and any other data the inviting teacher would like to share.

In the pre-conference, the inviting teacher has the opportunity to "unpack" her thinking about the lesson to be taught. To facilitate this, the coach asks questions that cause the teacher to reflect on the planning process that preceded the lesson; sometimes the teacher may express concern about a particular aspect of the lesson. One teacher said to her coach, "I am struggling with how to help 3rd grade students understand the properties of multiplication and the relationship between multiplication and division." The coach responded by asking, "Could you share with me what your preliminary plan is?" This inquiry began a dialogue that engaged the teacher and the coach in reflecting on past experiences teaching the concept, successes and challenges, and the unique learning profiles of the students that year. The coach shared an online video example with the teacher. Together, they reworked the lesson and created a contingency plan in case students' behavior indicated they were having difficulty meeting the desired lesson outcome in the middle of the teaching session. These interactions augmented the resources the teacher could tap, modeled a thought process of recalling past successes that she could follow if she ran into challenges in the future when the coach was not present, and developed a shared investment in the lesson. The coach was able to experience the impact of questioning strategies on the teacher's thinking and problem-solving strategies, and developed a sense of ownership in the lesson as a consequence of coplanning.

The pre-conference also gives the coach an opportunity to ask the inviting teacher about the lesson's desired outcome, its purpose, teaching strategies to be used, desired student behaviors, and the lesson context (what preceded the lesson, what will follow, whether the lesson is an introduction, a review, or an extended practice session). In addition, as noted earlier, the inviting teacher identifies a desired focus for the observation. Usually the focus is something the teacher has been working on or is curious about. The notion is that the coach can provide another set of eyes or a different perspective on what is transpiring in the classroom. The coach's work needs to be guided by the teacher so that the observational data are meaningful. The teacher specifies how data are to be collected, and often a sample observation tool is sketched out. In other cases, the teacher may ask that the lesson be video-recorded with a tablet or a digital camera. (Chapter 6 addresses additional issues affecting the observation process and methods of observing and collecting data.)

Clarifying the coach's role is another important decision that is made during the pre-conference. The teacher and the coach agree on things such as whether the coach will sit, stand, or move, whether the coach is to interact with students, and where the coach will physically be located in the room throughout the lesson. Some teachers have developed a signal to give to the coach if, during the course of the lesson, the teacher wishes the coach to leave.

At the conclusion of the pre-conference, the coach offers a summary of his understanding of the lesson, the observation task, and the agreements and the parameters for the observation. The inviting

teacher provides feedback as to the accuracy of the coach's understandings and clarifies any misinterpretations or misconceptions. Teacher
and coach confirm the date of and time frame for the observation.
At the conclusion of the pre-conference, the coach asks for feedback:
"Would you give me some feedback about the coaching process we
used today? Which questions activated your reflection and thinking?
What was useful? Was there anything I asked or did that you wished I
would have done differently?"

Usually, the pre-conference takes 20 to 40 minutes. In some cases
it may take an hour if the lesson is replanned or resources are needed.
Conferencing should take place in an area where both teacher and
coach are comfortable.

The language the coach uses to formulate the pre-conference questions should address the areas described in the preceding paragraphs
but should not seem like a formula. Often a teacher's response to a
coach's question takes the conversation in a needed direction, but not
one that was anticipated. That sort of thing *should* happen. The coaching conversation should be free-flowing and serve both Peer Coaching
partners by achieving the following goals:

- Building trust, understanding, and rapport;
- Promoting rehearsal and reflection about the lesson;
- Gathering information about the standard being addressed or the
lesson outcome(s);
- Eliciting information about the lesson's purpose or meaning and
about the skills embedded in the lesson;
- Collecting information about the desired teaching behaviors;
- Generating data about how students will be engaged throughout
the lesson;
- Identifying how student understanding or mastery will be
assessed;
- Reviewing the lesson context;
- Anticipating teacher concerns, challenges, or questions;
- Determining the role of the coach;
- Clarifying the observation focus;

• Deciding how data will be collected; sketching an example or ensuring that technology is functioning well, if it will be used;

• Summarizing the understanding of the lesson and the data-collection process;

• Identifying the date and time frame of the observation, and if possible, the date and time for the post-conference; and

• Providing an opportunity for the coach to receive feedback about the coaching strategies and process.

It's All About the Questions

Many teachers learning conferencing skills say that the most difficult part of the coaching process is determining which questions to ask and how to word them. This is true! There is no recipe for asking questions. If there were, the questions would seem stilted and not reflective of the personality style of the individual asking them. Rather, the coach asks an opening question, and the teacher's response is used to generate the next question. Figure 5.1 (p. 75) illustrates the decisions that influence the flow of possible questions based on the teacher's responses.

To develop fluency, teachers often practice formulating questions based on the goals of the pre-conference. (Appendix B contains examples of questions used by some Peer Coaching partners to practice developing pre-conference questions.) In some situations, when time to meet is scarce or schedules don't align, the teacher and the coach e-mail one another or use Skype to address pre-conference questions and establish the desired focus for the observation.

Communication Skills

How questions are asked is just as important as which questions are asked. The words chosen and the tone with which the words are delivered have a profound effect on how both parties—teacher and coach—will embrace the coaching process. Developing sensitivity to the tone of the conversation during the conferencing process—and

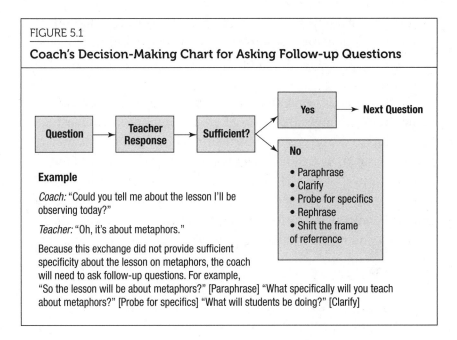

FIGURE 5.1

Coach's Decision-Making Chart for Asking Follow-up Questions

Question → Teacher Response → Sufficient?

Yes → Next Question

No
- Paraphrase
- Clarify
- Probe for specifics
- Rephrase
- Shift the frame of referrence

Example

Coach: "Could you tell me about the lesson I'll be observing today?"

Teacher: "Oh, it's about metaphors."

Because this exchange did not provide sufficient specificity about the lesson on metaphors, the coach will need to ask follow-up questions. For example, "So the lesson will be about metaphors?" [Paraphrase] "What specifically will you teach about metaphors?" [Probe for specifics] "What will students be doing?" [Clarify]

even in informal interactions within the halls of the school—can be a helpful awareness. It has the potential to contribute immensely to Peer Coaching's success. Word choice can enhance or inhibit conversations about teaching and learning. Whenever possible, avoid jargon. Doing a background interview with a coaching colleague can yield important insights regarding communication patterns and preferences. One coach and veteran teacher offered the following reflection:

> I asked the inviting teacher, "How do you feel the planning process went?" She just stared at me and finally responded, "I didn't *feel* anything about it, but I can tell you how I *think* it went." I know this example sounds kind of weird, but the interaction increased my understanding of the power of words and how we each present ourselves to the world. I am a feeler, but I was definitely working with a person who processes experiences using thinking skills. Her response caught me off guard, but it definitely influenced the language I chose in future coaching interactions.

We laugh about that now. The lesson we learned really enhanced the quality of our interactions. (Personal communication from a veteran teacher in Kentucky, April 2013)

The coach and the inviting teacher are continually making intentional choices about verbal and nonverbal communication. Making good choices leads to creating an environment of emotional and psychological safety that facilitates the cognitive complexity of the coaching conversation, the clarity with which communication occurs, and the depth of thinking that emerges for examining one's practices and their consequences. Throughout the conferencing process, the following communication skills (adapted from Costa & Garmston, 2002) have been found to be helpful:

• *Silence or "wait time"* provides time for both partners to think or reflect.

• *Paraphrasing or active listening* are strategies that allow an opportunity to check for understanding to see if a message was received as it was intended by the sender.

• *Clarifying* helps determine if the communication was understood or misconceived.

• *Pressing for specificity* invites elaboration and more precise information and details.

• *Avoiding negatives embedded in a message* helps ensure that the receiver is not put off or emotionally hijacked and can focus on what is being discussed. (For example, saying "Can you think of another way you could have taught the lesson?" conveys a message that one might lack the ability to do this. Instead, consider asking questions such as "What is your hunch about why some students performed as you envisioned they would and others did not?")

• *Reframing* shifts the point of reference to consider the question from a different perspective. (For example, if a person says, "I wish I could have used more technology in this lesson to actively engage students," the coach may enable the teacher to think of additional internal resources by asking, "Has there been a time in the past in a different lesson when you used technology to foster students' active engagement? If so, would any of those strategies work in this lesson?")

• *Neutral comments or assertions* help create rapport.

Teachers who have used these communication tools as they conferenced reported that they think more comprehensively about their own teaching—before, during, and after instruction—as well as that of their colleagues. They also note that the conferencing process and use of communication skills enable them to think critically and creatively—a practice they are working to instill in their students.

The pre-conference experience creates bonds between and among staff members, adding to the collegiality in a school. "When people engage in rich conversations, it changes the culture to one of collective efficacy," notes Laura Lipton (in Armstrong, 2012, p. 5). The act of coaching inspires teachers to talk with one another, to learn from one another, to see each other as resources, and to value others' perspectives. Collectively, these outcomes contribute to building the capacity to improve practice in a way that leaves its mark on the teaching profession and its propensity to produce student learning.

Summary

Successful conferencing requires both relationship skills, including the ability to build trust, and technical expertise, such as knowing how to develop and pose appropriate questions and how to listen effectively. The work of Judith Warren Little suggests six principles for effective conferencing, which fall into two categories: technical (common language, focus, and hard evidence); and social (interaction, predictability, and reciprocity). Costa and Garmston's Cognitive Coaching model informs the goals of conferencing, with the ultimate goal being teacher autonomy.

The pre-conference provides essential groundwork for the lesson observation to follow. The coach asks the inviting teacher questions about the intended outcomes of the lesson, characteristics of the students, teaching strategies to be used, the desired focus, parameters, and data collection method for the observation. Though the coach may ask questions, the inviting teacher decides the focus and methods to be used in the observation. The coach's questioning skills—including the manner in which questions are asked—are key to a successful pre-conference. Both the inviting teacher and the coach make intentional choices about verbal and nonverbal communication, and these choices contribute to the creation of a climate characterized by mutual trust. The impact of the pre-conference on teachers' skillfulness in the classroom, as well as in the coaching role, adds to the capacity of the culture to serve the needs of staff and students. Chapter 6 will focus on strategies to ensure a skillful observation.

Reflective Questions

1. After reading the section entitled Six Principles for Effective Conferencing (pp. 67–69) that detailed technical expertise and relationship skills needed for conferencing, which principles do you believe are more influential in the coaching process? Which do you believe are the most difficult to develop? Why?

2. What are some activities a coach and an inviting teacher could engage in to increase the fluency with which pre-conference questions are generated?

3. In addition to the communication skills listed in this chapter, what others might you add?

4. Thinking about the school in which you work, how could the schedule be arranged to facilitate quality time for the pre-conference?

6

Ensuring a Skillful Observation

It's inspiring to watch someone else practice their craft. It is a great form of professional development that causes me to reflect upon my own practices as well as serve a colleague.

—Peer Coach, Sewickley Academy, Sewickley, Pa.

The observation process affords the inviting teacher "another set of eyes" with which to examine her classroom. Robbins & Alvy (2014) emphasize that "the primary purpose of the observation is to provide data from instructional episodes and student work samples for reflection following the lesson and for discussion during the post-conference" (p. 140).

Focusing the Observation

As discussed in Chapter 5, the parameters for the observation are established by the inviting teacher during the pre-conference. The teacher should decide the focus of the observation and how data are to be collected so that the coach collects data that are meaningful and useful in the teacher's quest to maximize the effect of instruction on student learning. Some teachers report, however, that one of the most difficult aspects of Peer Coaching, after conquering feelings of discomfort about teaching publicly, is deciding on a focus for the observation. This is the case, one teacher hypothesized, because classroom observation has been historically tied to evaluation. And those evaluation observations were steered either by an evaluation instrument used by the principal or by a particular instructional or curricular approach taught during a professional development session. Having the latitude to choose the focus for oneself can be overwhelming.

In response to this concern, peer coaches in one school decided to develop an electronic menu of options from which the inviting teacher could select a focus for the observation. It looked like a restaurant menu and included options that peer partners had brainstormed, such as teacher-student interactions, critical thinking skills, transitions, wait time, student engagement, instructional strategies, blended learning, use of digital devices, verbal flow, teacher proximity, a particular student or small group, pacing, student understanding, and student work.

Because Peer Coaching activities should not be evaluative, some of the menu topics would require that the coach ask the teacher for guidelines so that the data could be collected without judgment. Let's suppose, for example, that the teacher asked the coach to focus on the pacing of the lesson. To avoid being evaluative, the coach would have to ask the teacher, "If pacing was appropriate, what should I expect to see?" The teacher would then reflect on indicators of appropriate pacing, articulate those to the coach, and the coach could simply collect data about the presence or absence of these indicators, without interpretation.

It is easy to draw on opinions and conclusions when observing, but what really helps a teacher is evidence and description. In *Crucial Conversations*, Patterson, Grenny, McMillan, & Switzler (2002) advise us to "separate fact from story by focusing on behavior... can you *see* or *hear* this thing you are calling a fact? What was the actual behavior?" (p. 105). Also, it is essential that the observation be focused on something the inviting teacher genuinely cares about, believes is important, or finds perplexing. It should be a variable that in some way affects professional practice and student learning. It should also be an element that the teacher can influence.

Another factor that affects the selection of a focus for the observation is the teacher's comfort level with the coach. If peer partners have not worked together for any length of time, many wonder, "How do I measure up in the eyes of my colleague?" Because of this uneasiness, the inviting teacher may select a focus for the observation that is safe—something the teacher is confident about and does well. For example, one teacher asked her coach to record the way in which she distributed her proximity among students in the classroom by creating an image of the student desks and other furniture and just drawing lines to illustrate her movement among students. The coach adhered to this focus, but as he began to observe, he realized that using color to illustrate increments of time would add a valuable dimension to data collection, so he chose to color code the lines he drew. He made a key that represented time increments with different colors. The first five minutes, he used blue to record teacher movement among students; the second five minutes, he used green, and so on. After the observation, when he met for the post-conference, he first asked the teacher to recall where she had spent time in the classroom throughout the lesson. After the teacher reflected upon this, he shared the data he had collected. She expressed surprise at first, seeing the colors. But then she began noticing and describing patterns she observed. This was the turning point in the conference—and in their coach-teacher relationship. The interaction created a trust in the observation process that led to further productive coaching sessions.

As trust builds between the coach and the teacher, and the two have the opportunity to switch coaching roles, the inviting teacher may be more willing to take risks, experiment, and "let his or her rough edges show" (Little, 1981). These "rough edges" give them something to hang onto as they examine the practice and consequences of teaching. Coaching should be a dynamic process. Not only should the coaching partners have the opportunity to switch roles, but the focus of the observations should be able to change as the inviting teacher wishes.

Communicating About the Observation with Students

Before an observation, the inviting teacher usually tells students about the coach's scheduled visit. A teacher might explain to the class, "Today Ms. Cubbage will be coming in to watch our class. She is interested in what helps us learn. At another time, I will visit her classroom. In this school, teachers believe in learning from one another." Many Peer Coaching partners have commented that using statements such as these affords them an opportunity to model collaborative work with adults for their students, similar to the cooperative learning strategies they are implementing in their classrooms.

Tips and Resources for Observing

What takes place during a classroom observation is influenced by the experience of the inviting teacher and the coach, their relationship, the presence of trust, and the context of the classroom or school in which the observation takes place. Peer Coaching partners are constantly striving to expand their repertoires of observation tools and strategies. The following tips are intended to generate additional ideas to enhance the observation process.

Using the Student Learning Nexus model. It is useful for Peer Coaching partners to have a model related to teaching and learning that illuminates the complexities of lessons. The Student Learning Nexus, developed by Alvy and Robbins and shown in Figure 6.1 (p. 83), presents a way to examine the interrelationships between classroom environment, instruction, curriculum, and assessment, as they relate to student learning. Coaching partners can use it as a resource to identify an observation focus, or a framework for examining the interplay of specific elements. In essence, it is a tool to explore a lesson and enrich the conversation about teaching and learning.

Understanding the concept of visible learning. John Hattie's book *Visible Learning for Teachers* (2012a) has informed the work of many teachers engaged in coaching activities. Hattie asserts the following:

FIGURE 6.1

The Student Learning Nexus: Balancing Curriculum, Instruction, and Assessment in a Healthy School Culture

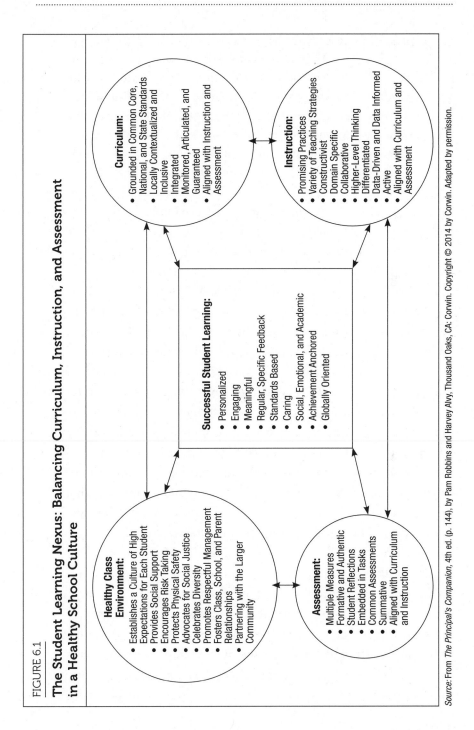

Curriculum:
- Grounded in Common Core, National, and State Standards
- Locally Contextualized and Inclusive
- Integrated
- Monitored, Articulated, and Guaranteed
- Aligned with Instruction and Assessment

Instruction:
- Promising Practices
- Variety of Teaching Strategies
- Constructivist
- Domain Specific
- Collaborative
- Higher-Level Thinking
- Differentiated
- Data-Driven and Data Informed
- Active
- Aligned with Curriculum and Assessment

Successful Student Learning:
- Personalized
- Engaging
- Meaningful
- Regular, Specific Feedback
- Standards Based
- Caring
- Social, Emotional, and Academic
- Achievement Anchored
- Globally Oriented

Healthy Class Environment:
- Establishes a Culture of High Expectations for Each Student
- Provides Social Support
- Encourages Risk Taking
- Protects Physical Safety
- Advocates for Social Justice
- Celebrates Diversity
- Promotes Respectful Management
- Fosters Class, School, and Parent Relationships
- Partnering with the Larger Community

Assessment:
- Multiple Measures
- Formative and Authentic
- Student Reflections
- Embedded in Tasks
- Common Assessments
- Summative
- Aligned with Curriculum and Instruction

Source: From *The Principal's Companion,* 4th ed. (p. 144), by Pam Robbins and Harvey Alvy, Thousand Oaks, CA: Corwin. Copyright © 2014 by Corwin. Adapted by permission.

I never allow teachers or school leaders to visit classrooms to observe teachers; I allow them to observe only students—the reactions that students have to incidents, to teaching, to peers, to the activity. Then they interview and listen to the student about what the student was doing, thinking, not understanding. Such observation adds another pair of eyes to help the teacher to see the effect of his or her teaching, and moves the discussion away from the teaching toward the *effect* of the teaching. (p. 155)

The point that student feedback to the teacher makes learning visible is a notion that has resonated with coaching partners and underscores the importance of collecting observational data that includes evidence of student learning such as students' responses and artifacts of student work. The idea that student "mistakes" and verbal reflections can become a source for improving teaching and can offer important direction for making midcourse adjustments is compelling. Many teachers have mentioned how this approach totally changed the way they looked at learning in their own classrooms and in their colleagues' classrooms, and how it served as a talking point in the post-conference.

Focusing on student work. Collecting student work during an observation creates the opportunity for teachers, during the post-conference, to connect their planning for a lesson, teaching that lesson, and expected outcomes with the evidence of learning that students produce. Phil Schlechty (2001) states, "Teachers do not cause learning... Rather, they design activities for students from which students will learn" (p. 83). He advises that rather than focusing on the teaching during a classroom observation, it is valuable to focus on students "to determine the extent to which students are engaged, persist, and experience a sense of accomplishment and satisfaction as a result of what they are asked to do" (p. 144). Making sure that the "right work" is assigned is essential. In fact, Schlechty believes that "the primary source of variance in student learning is the quality of the work the teachers and the schools provide to students" (p. 84). Many coaching partners appreciate this view and have said the focus on the student eases the teacher's self-consciousness, while providing valuable evidence. Some inviting teachers routinely bring student work from the lesson that was observed to the post-conference. Questions about the effect of the lesson on student learning are often clarified and answered as the coach and the inviting teacher review the students' work.

Including the students' voices. Collecting the words of students, either through scripting or by video-recording them during the observation, adds an important dimension to the data available to the coach and the teacher during the post-conference. Donald Schön (1987) writes,

> When a teacher turns her attention to... listening to what [kids] say, then teaching becomes a form of *reflection-in-action*, and I think this formulation helps to describe what it is that constitutes teaching artistry. It involves getting in touch with what kids are actually saying and doing; it involves allowing yourself to be surprised by that, and allowing yourself to be surprised... is appropriate because you must permit yourself to be surprised, being puzzled by what you get and responding to the puzzle through an on-the-spot experiment that you make, that responds to what the kid says or does. It involves meeting the kid in the sense of meeting his or her understanding of what is going on, and helping the kid coordinate the everyday *knowing-in-action* that he brings to the school with the privileged knowledge that he finds at school.

An inviting teacher asked his coach to record the conversations of two groups that were working independently while he worked with another. During the post-conference, the inviting teacher expressed amazement with the conversations about character and plot that the coach captured during the observation. He indicated that he had no idea about the self-help measures students were using to access information, or how well they were using the listening skills, paraphrasing techniques, and clarifying strategies, that he had taught them. The teacher also collaborated with the coach about how to add depth to the discussions of the small, independent groups.

Collecting observational data with digital devices. Technology has enabled coaches to conveniently collect classroom data during the observation and share it with the inviting teacher during the post-conference. Smartphones, laptops, tablets, and digital video cameras can help the coach to capture parts of the lesson (e.g., beginning, middle, and end), teacher-student interactions, small-group dialogue, student performance, and other facets of the lesson about which the inviting teacher has expressed curiosity. There are many applications to choose from, but beware! If the application does the synopsis or creates the summary, it may detract from the possibility of a rich analysis conversation that could take place during the coaching session.

Educators George Manthey and Jeanie Cash developed an application for the iPad called Videre (also mentioned in Chapter 1), which enables the coach to digitally record a lesson and then review it and mark clips of the video with a label. The preset labels include such things as collaborating, communicating, creating, examples of learning, feedback, metacognition, and thinking critically; and it is possible to add additional categories or change the preset ones. Labeling clips that align with the desired focus of the inviting teacher can save valuable time in the post-conference. Or, if the teacher prefers, the coach and the inviting teacher can review the video and categorize clips together. One teacher reflected, "A 10-minute lesson segment can lead to a 45-minute dialogue about this objective video! My coach and I are both growing professionally, and our students will reap the benefits!"

Clarifying agreements. Recently, a coach, Dania Paul, offered the following advice:

> Be specific and ask questions about the desired observation focus in the pre-conference. Whether you are the person making the observation or the one being observed, you want to be certain that both parties understand what you are specifically looking for. It also minimizes the stress of the observation. Keep it confidential—it's important that the observation stays between the two parties involved—whether it was a fabulous lesson or not, confidentiality is a must.

The coach must collect data without judgment, sticking to the agreements made in the pre-conference.

Data Collection

It is essential that the inviting teacher and the coach talk about the data-collection instrument or method in detail during the pre-conference so that the data collected during the observation match the desired focus. As mentioned earlier, data can be collected digitally or by hand. Despite the availability of commercial data-collection forms and instruments, most coaches and inviting teachers prefer to create their own so that they can tailor the method to their specific needs.

Because of the variety of ways to collect data for a particular focus, Peer Coaching partners should discuss options and even sketch their ideas out before making a final decision. When this does not happen, the coach may collect data in a way that he thinks was specified by the teacher, when in fact the inviting teacher may have had a completely different notion in mind. Recently, for example, a coach was asked to collect data about the questions the inviting teacher asked students, the wait time that followed each question, and the student responses. The inviting teacher requested that this be done manually instead of digitally because she thought the video would distract students. The coach thought she understood how data were to be collected, so she did not sketch out any details. Before the observation, the coach created a document that looked like this:

Teacher Questions	Wait Time	Student Name/Response

When the lesson began, however, the coach realized that the teacher asked a question that required critical thinking, then waited so students could think, then called on a student, but didn't stop there. After the student responded, the teacher waited, and then asked,

"Would anyone like to add to this response, or perhaps you had a different response?" And then the teacher waited again! So the coach modified the data-collection format to resemble this pattern. She actually had to rotate the legal pad of paper she was using and record the data horizontally to accommodate the increased number of columns:

Teacher Question	Wait Time	Student Name/ Response	Wait Time	Teacher Question	Wait Time	Student Name/ Response

The coach was feeling a bit stressed because she had to change the data-collection strategy in the middle of the lesson to align how she was collecting data with the inviting teacher's request. And in making the adjustment, she missed capturing a few of the teacher's questions. In the post-conference, the coach asked the teacher to recall her questions, use of wait time, and student responses. Then the coach explained how she had to modify the data-collection form mid-lesson and confessed that she missed recording a few questions.

As the coach displayed the data, the teacher fell silent and pored over the information. The coach sat quietly, worrying that she had overwhelmed or disappointed the teacher. Suddenly the teacher said, "Look at this pattern! I called on some kids first, while others I consistently called on in second position, when I asked, 'Would anyone like to add to that?' So the kids I always called on second had more time to think. And look at their answers. They are much more complex!" The coach was relieved and intrigued by this response, and indicated that the teacher had seen something in the data that she had missed. Together they discussed what they learned from this experience. The teacher requested that the coach observe again and expressed a desire to vary the order in which she called on students. They also decided to collaboratively develop the observation instrument they would use.

One data-collection method that many teachers have found comfortable working with is the Verbal Flow Chart (Figure 6.2). This chart illustrates to whom the teacher spoke and which students responded during an observation period. To create this chart, the coach simply draws boxes to represent each student and a circle to represent the teacher. Each time the teacher speaks to the class, an arrow is drawn from the circle to the class. When specific students are addressed, arrows pointing toward the student are drawn in their

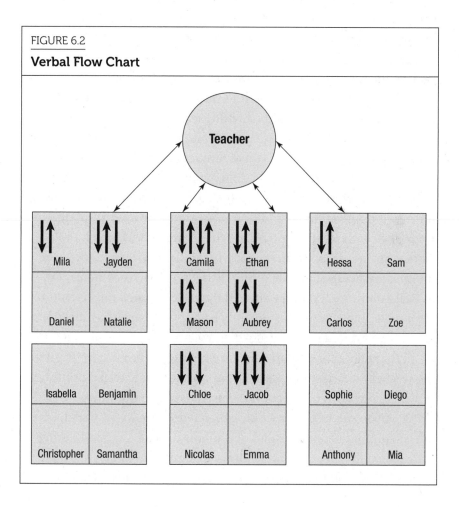

FIGURE 6.2

Verbal Flow Chart

boxes. If students respond, arrows are drawn in their boxes pointing to the teacher. Although this approach yields information about the frequency of the interactions between the teacher and the entire class, as well as specific students, it does not provide information about the quality of the questions, student engagement, or the order of these interactions. Some coaches have used color coding to indicate the order of these interactions (e.g., first question from the teacher in red, with student interaction responses in red, second question in blue, etc.). Despite the limitations of this observation instrument, the teacher can use the information collected to quickly assess which students were called on, which students had the most interaction, and which students were overlooked. This instrument can be hand drawn or created as a template on a laptop or tablet device. Admittedly, a video could capture the same interactions; however, it would take longer to review.

Another data-collection method is called scripting. The coach simply writes or types what the inviting teacher says and does, and what students say and do during all or part of a lesson. Then the data become part of the coaching conversation during the post-conference. Some coaches find this method difficult, but others find it valuable. Recently an inviting teacher asked the coach to focus on transitions during an observation. In addition to scripting the lesson and directions, the coach went one step further and timed how long it took students to transition from one activity to the next. This allowed the inviting teacher to study the prompts that preceded each transition, as well as how each prompt affected the time required for students to respond and the nature of student behavior. Although the transitions could have been digitally recorded and viewed, having a written transcript for analysis and future reference is a useful resource for the inviting teacher. In fact, some teachers and coaches have created portfolios in which they keep observation artifacts to refer to over time.

A person's style and processing preferences (auditory, visual, or kinesthetic) influence decisions about how data are captured during the observation. Several online forms are available—a quick Google search yields many examples of peer-observation forms. Many forms have a checklist format, however, which prompts a cautionary note: a simple check mark is efficient and can indicate presence or absence of an attribute but it often does not portray the quality of what is being examined. Further, checklists leave little to talk about. Qualitative data such as scripting, teacher and coach designed forms, or video recordings create a richer source of data to draw from in the post-conference.

Data collection using digital devices certainly expands the options available to coaching partners. It is important to collaboratively explore the desired focus for the observation before selecting the digital device to capture that information. In addition, it is important that the students in the class being observed be prepared for the visit so that data collection does not distract them. Although digital devices can reduce the time it takes to collect data, watching a video of an entire lesson can be time consuming. Therefore, some coaching partners decide on a narrow focus, such as openings, practice sessions, and closings. In other examples of practice, the inviting teacher reviews the video first and selects the parts she desires to discuss with the coach. Possibilities abound. Decisions about how to digitally collect data will reflect preferences for focusing the observation and be influenced by how much time is available for the observation and post-conference. A word of caution is also in order here. Applications have been developed for the major instructional frameworks and specific topics such as student responses, Bloom's taxonomy, cooperative learning, time on task, wait time, student behavior, quality of teacher directions, and more. Some of these applications can create attractive bar graphs and pie charts. However, if the information recorded is not accessible in a format that invites intellectual inquiry and analysis, as well as two-way reflective dialogue about teaching and learning, the data are not worth collecting—no matter how cool the application is.

Observational data should be specific, not general, and objective, not interpretive. The data-collection method should match the teacher's desired focus for the observation, be negotiated in detail by coach and teacher, reflect the teacher's style and preferences, and be a manageable task for the coach. Decisions about whether to use technology in the data-collection process should reflect the needs of the coaching partners and the unique characteristics of the context in which the observation is to occur. Reflecting on the value of the observation experience, one teacher proclaimed, "This type of observation is so helpful. Because we are not being evaluated, it can simply raise our awareness. We become better teachers when we are aware."

Summary

The primary purpose of the observation process is to provide data for discussion during the post-conference. The inviting teacher decides what the focus of the observation will be; a menu of options may help individuals new to the coaching process select a meaningful focus. It is essential that the data collected during the observation be objective, be useful in its role of facilitating reflection on practice, and have the capacity to inspire conversations. Resources and tips for data collection include the introduction of the Student Learning Nexus model, John Hattie's concept of "visible learning," the need to include student work and student voices in data collection, and the use of digital devices, which afford both opportunities and challenges for data collection. Skillful data collection during the observation process will lay the groundwork for a productive post-conference experience, which is the focus of Chapter 7.

Reflective Questions

1. Which observation tools resonated with you? What additional ones would you add?

2. To begin or extend a conversation about the observation process, consider inviting professional colleagues at your school to create a T chart on which they list possible areas of focus on the left, and how this data may be collected on the right.

3. In what ways might student work serve as an observation arti-
fact? How has student work been used in the past to inform practice by
professionals at your school?

4. What are some unique variables in your school that may impact
data collection?

7

Inviting Reflection Through the Post-Conference

Our conversations invent us.

—Harriet Lerner, psychologist and author of
The Dance of Connection (2001, p. 239)

The post-conference creates an opportunity for the inviting teacher and the coach to reflect on a lesson that has been observed in relation to the expected and actual outcomes and to make sense of the results. Questions posed by the coach begin a conversation that cultivates reflection and the germination of insights and new ideas, as well as the opportunity to create new knowledge about one's practice. As a consequence of this rich interchange, the inviting teacher consciously refines teaching practices and invents new ways of providing learning experiences with the goal of increasing student learning. The coach develops and refines questioning strategies that assist the inviting teacher in discovering which instructional approaches have the most profound influence on teaching and learning.

How the Post-Conference Works

After the observation, both the inviting teacher and the coach usually reflect individually on the lesson that has been observed. When they come together in the post-conference, often the inviting teacher eagerly opens the conversation by sharing thoughts or feelings. However, in some cases, the inviting teacher may look to the coach to begin the conversation, in which case the coach may pose an open-ended question to elicit the teacher's feelings or thoughts about the lesson—for example, "How do you feel or think the lesson went?" After the teacher responds, the coach may invite the teacher to reflect on the lesson to uncover the source of these feelings or to trace the series of events that promoted these thoughts. If the teacher's reflections align with the designated focus for the observation, the coach then shares the data collected. Strategically, the coach invites the teacher to unpack her recollections before sharing the data so that the data do not bias the teacher's recollections. At this point, the teacher may compare her perceptions with the evidence provided by the coach. Together, they discuss any similarities or differences between the teacher's perceptions and the evidence.

However, sometimes the inviting teacher, in response to the coach's opening question, may bring up aspects of the lesson that do not pertain to the focus that was decided upon in the pre-conference. If this happens, the coach may say, "Although this was not the focus you asked me to collect data on in the pre-conference, I am willing to reflect on this with you if that is your preference." Many times, the teacher will simply say, "I just needed to air those thoughts and feelings. Let's refocus on what I asked you to look for." On other occasions, the teacher may ask the coach to divert from the original focus and spend time on whatever is occupying the teacher's thoughts at that moment.

The overarching goal of the post-conference is for the coach to ask the inviting teacher questions that promote reflection about the lesson and analysis of what happened as expected and what happened differently. In addition, the teacher is often asked to project, if she were to teach the lesson again, what she would replicate and what she would do differently, and why. The reference point for this dialogue and analysis is always about the effect of teaching on student learning. The coach's approach might be thought of as one that invites discrepancy analysis. It is the teacher who articulates the goals of the lesson in the pre-conference and then decides—based on a recollection of the lesson, student performance data, and the coach's data—whether or not the lesson produced student learning. The teacher should have an opportunity to verbalize a comparison between her recollections of the lesson and the actual data from the observation. If the lesson resulted in student learning, it is important to understand what specifically caused that learning to occur so the teacher can repeat those strategies in future lessons. If the lesson did not result in student learning, the coach and the teacher invoke a problem-solving approach, as if they had joined together to discover why the expectations for performance were not met. For example, analyzing errors in student work can yield powerful insights about why students were not able to reach mastery and what interventions should be implemented. John Hattie (2012b) notes, "Gathering and assessing feedback are really the only ways teachers can know the impact of their teaching… When teachers listen to their students' learning, they know what worked, what didn't, and what they need to change to foster student growth" (p. 23).

The coach plays a critical role in facilitating these understandings. Having been invited to reflect on and analyze the lesson, the teacher has the opportunity to explore cause-effect relationships between teaching behaviors and desired student outcomes. The coaching experience allows the teacher to reconstruct a lesson and analyze its effects. This builds within the teacher a knowledge base that will inform future lessons. One group of teachers who had been participating together in formal coaching for a semester offered the following observations:

> Becoming aware of how to use nonevaluative language was one of the most difficult facets of our coaching training to apply.… Learning about how to collect data and generate questions that cause your colleagues to reflect and think about their thinking, their actions, and the consequences is a critical aspect of the coaching. It is inspiring to ask a question and observe how that question can cause your colleague to alter his or her perspective. It is amazing to behold the value of silence as a dimension of the feedback process. It gives both the coach and the teacher precious time to think.

The post-conference usually concludes with the coach asking the inviting teacher for specific feedback about conferencing skills. For instance, the coach might ask, "Would you give me some feedback about the conferencing skills I used today? What did I do that facilitated your thinking? Was there anything you wished I had done differently?" Asking such questions allows the coach to further develop conferencing skills, and it models the reciprocity discussed in Chapter 4 that contributes to the development of trust among professional colleagues. One coach reflected, after the inviting teacher provided feedback about his coaching strategies, "I have learned powerful lessons about questioning strategies, the use of silence, responding behaviors, and tools to promote metacognition—thinking about thinking—and supporting colleagues in generating next steps, just by asking for feedback." Another factor that contributes to building trust is the coach's commitment to adhere to focusing only on those areas specified by the inviting teacher. As mentioned in Chapter 4, at the very end of the post-conference, the coach hands the observation data to the inviting teacher, as well as any artifacts of student work that were collected during the observation. Symbolically, this is an important act. It separates coaching from evaluation. The inviting teacher ultimately chooses what to do with the data.

Although the coach's obligation to stick to commitments of serving the inviting teacher is important, there is one exception. In rare cases, when a coach has observed students being put at risk—emotionally, psychologically, or physically—the coach has a moral and ethical obligation to address the issue with the teacher and, if need be, the school principal. Students *always* come first.

Post-Conference Questions and Goals

The questioning strategies used by the coach during the post-conference should be tailored to what the coach knows and understands about the inviting teacher (thinker versus feeler, introvert versus extrovert, processing preferences, and personality style). This sensitivity and

awareness maximizes rapport and provides a foundation for open dialogue about teaching and learning. It also influences the way questions
are posed. Consider the following questions:

- How do you think the lesson went?
- How do you feel the lesson went?
- Did it go as you hoped?
- Did you achieve the goals you had for this lesson?

As you read through the questions, did some resonate with you more
than others? Because individuals are sensitive to language and tone,
rather than have scripted questions, the coach's questions should be
developed from goals articulated in the pre-conference and in the
observation experiences so that they can reflect the unique interchange
between a coach and the inviting teacher. As mentioned in Chapter 5
and illustrated in the decision-making chart presented in Figure 5.1,
after a coach asks the inviting teacher a question, the coach's follow-up
question should take into account the teacher's response. Therefore,
questions do not follow an implicit order. (Appendix B offers sample
questions that could be used in the post-conference.)

The following list of goals can shape and inform questions asked
during the post-conference:

- Promote teacher reflection on the lesson by
  - Recalling one's own behavior and the behaviors of students.
  - Comparing the actual behaviors that occurred during the
    lesson with those expected.
  - Analyzing why behaviors were or were not performed (factors
    that may have influenced the results).
  - Making inferences about the achievement of the lesson's pur-
    pose/standard/objective (analysis of evidence to support one's
    impressions or judgments).
  - Generalizing about new ideas or connections about students,
    curriculum, instruction, assignments, or assessments that have
    developed as a result of this teaching episode.

- Create future plans by
    - Establishing new goals for oneself, students, student work, and future lessons as a result of teaching this lesson.
    - Generating and integrating new ideas, understandings, and skills that will inform future lessons.
    - Planning next steps for instruction and curriculum.
    - Designing student work, performance tasks, and rubrics.

- Provide feedback about practices for the inviting teacher and coach.

- Create motivation to participate in future Peer Coaching opportunities.

Many coaching partners have developed future lessons together as a result of their joint work during the post-conference. Sometimes they switch roles: coach becomes inviting teacher and inviting teacher becomes coach. Their work often reflects a particular professional learning focus in which they share a mutual interest. Many coaches and inviting teachers have developed portfolios or logs about their experiences so that they can intentionally build on their learnings from past coaching episodes. One coach reflected, "This has been such a valuable learning experience for me. I fear I have learned more than I provided to my colleague. I am more aware of my own instructional decision making and what fosters learning as a consequence of observing a peer."

Coaches' Reflections

Experienced coaches are an excellent source of insight into the coaching process. Here are reflections from several different coaches, with varying levels of experience:

It's tricky. It is difficult at times to represent what you heard or saw objectively, without judgment. It is important to capture the actual words of the teacher or students, or collect artifacts of classroom practice and student work to ensure that the data are judgment free. My motto has become, "Let the data talk."

It's new, and we need to be patient. We should look at ourselves as a work in progress—especially with respect to developing communication skills. We should give each other, as Peer Coaching partners, permission to take time when we are formulating questions or responding to a question.

It is so difficult not to say "great lesson" when what you see is truly amazing and you are overwhelmed with admiration for a colleague who has heightened the performance of students. But then I remind myself that "great" is a judgment, and Peer Coaching should not be evaluative. At that point, I have to turn inward and ask myself, "What caused the amazement and admiration?" If I can state those facts, I can deliver the same message, but without judgment. It is powerful, but such hard work!

The Peer Coaching process makes us aware of our practice. We are so busy, and the process creates time for metacognition. We become more aware of what each other is doing as well as what is going on in our building.

Peer Coaching experiences have made me realize that one's beliefs about learning, cognition, and emotion are interwoven into the fabric of our teaching. It is imperative that we interact with care. It is a delicate balance—being honest, acting with transparency about our practices, and making sure we don't hurt one another's feelings.

Meaningful conversations about curriculum, instruction, and assessment can rarely occur without evoking deeply held beliefs and philosophies. We have to be respectful of one another and put our ideas on the table to examine our practices without making people feel as if they are personally being dissected with their craft.

These coaches' reflections remind us how fragile the coaching process can be, especially when trust is first developing between professional colleagues. Even when the coach and inviting teacher have a history of working together, if agreements are broken, trust can disintegrate quickly. Further, for many professionals, teaching is an extension of one's self. Hence, when practices are examined, some individuals perceive that their professional selves are being questioned and dissected as well. Therefore, it is important to separate the practice of teaching from the person doing the teaching. An understanding of feedback can inform the work of coaching partners and contribute to the development of results-oriented practices that lead to staff and student learning.

Feedback

Research and practice emphasize that valued feedback and opportunities to use that feedback in a meaningful context enhance performance and achievement. Feedback involves conveying the effects of one's actions in relation to a goal. It can involve replaying a video of a lesson segment, reading a script of a teacher's words and student responses, or engaging the teacher in reflection in action as she observes student behavior generated within the context of a lesson. Although each of these feedback sources is different, they share common ground in that they are all judgment free. None carry within them any suggestions or recommendations.

Grant Wiggins (2012) offers this insight on what makes feedback helpful: "Whether feedback is just there to be grasped or is provided by another person, helpful feedback is goal-referenced; tangible and transparent; actionable; user-friendly (specific and personalized); timely; ongoing; and consistent" (p. 11). He points out that effective feedback requires that a person have a goal, act to achieve that particular goal, and receive information about whether the goal was addressed. With tangible information about the consequence of our performance, we can decide if the goal has been met or if alternative actions are indicated. The specificity of the feedback lends clarity to developing an action plan. For example, suppose the teacher says to the coach in a pre-conference, "I want the students to be highly engaged by the scenarios they are to investigate." The coach must ask a clarifying question so that he is not put in a position to render judgment about whether students were "highly engaged." To avoid being asked to evaluate "highly engaged," the coach might ask, "If the students are highly engaged, what will I see?" With this question, the coach causes the inviting teacher to ponder exactly what student behaviors she hopes the scenario activity will produce. When the teacher provides this clarification to the coach, then the coach simply collects feedback for the teacher about whether or not those behaviors were observed. Ultimately the inviting teacher, not the coach, makes the assessment about the goal being met, based on the feedback provided.

Feedback should be provided in a timely fashion so it can be acted upon. It may come from a coach, student work, or a digital record; but in all cases, what drives successful coaching is that the feedback is viewed as meaningful, goal referenced, acted upon, and consistently used to make midcourse adjustments. Inviting teachers and coaches come to value feedback because of its contribution to informing the next steps in instruction and coaching. And, because actions informed by feedback are strategic and results oriented, the outcomes are consistently of high quality. Educational consultant Laura Lipton adds, "Feedback that leads to growth and improvement is data-driven, is based on shared definitions and understandings between parties, acts as a foundation for conversation, and sets goals and improves practice by naming strengths and gaps in relation to a clear set of standards" (Armstrong, 2012, pp. 1–4).

Although feedback's value is well established, to have maximum effect on enhancing practice, it must be high quality, communicated objectively, consistent, and frequent. Thus coaching needs to take place more often than once a semester. Additionally, Carol Ann Tomlinson (2014) reminds us of the inherent need to differentiate feedback for teachers in the same way that we ask teachers to differentiate instruction for students in the classroom. Forms of feedback include the following:

- Written (based on data that the coach collects)
- Verbal (dialogue between coach and inviting teacher)

- Visual (video; snapshots)
- Auditory (recording)
- Student work
- Student voices
- Built into the task
- Invited versus imposed
- Reflective versus telling

How feedback is received is influenced by how it is communicated. Lipton (in Armstrong, 2012) notes that asking a question that begins with "Can you think of…" implies "potential doubt that the receiver can think of something. Instead, the question can be phrased as 'What might be some ways to…,' which invites exploration of the topic" (p. 4).

Providing feedback is based on certain assumptions, including the following:

- Ongoing inquiry and reflection are closely linked to improving practice.
- One size does not fit all; individualizing allows an avenue for responding to the different developmental and growth needs of staff.
- The focus of the feedback process is on building the capacity of staff members to serve students in a way that maximizes learning.
- The feedback process should focus on both relationship building and enhancing learning.

To be useful, feedback in conferences should have the following characteristics:

- Descriptive rather than evaluative,
- Specific rather than general,
- Responsive to the needs of both the receiver and the giver of the feedback,
- Directed toward behavior the receiver can change,
- Solicited rather than imposed,
- Well-timed, and
- Clearly understood by both the sender and the receiver.

Invited feedback about teaching provides teachers with data about the use of particular practices related to curriculum, instruction, assessment, social and emotional learning, and classroom management, as well as the consequences of those practices. The data provide a lens through which teachers can reflect on and examine their own behaviors in relation to their effect on student learning. The data also provide the basis for dialogue among professional colleagues about the thinking involved in planning and delivering instruction, and the effect on learning. Through the process of receiving feedback, teachers determine what they might do differently if they were to reteach the lesson. This careful analysis fosters professional growth, instructional excellence, and ultimately, student learning (Robbins & Alvy, 2014).

Feedback thrives and its effects are maximized when the environment in which it occurs is supportive. Such an environment is characterized by a shared belief that every individual within the culture of the school is capable of growing professionally, trust is present among all stakeholders, and a sense of psychological and emotional safety exists.

Summary

The post-conference provides an opportunity for the inviting teacher and the coach to share their reflections on the lesson that was observed, to examine the data collected, and to analyze the results. The goals for post-conferencing provide a framework from which the coach may develop questions, tailored to the unique characteristics of the inviting teacher and the context in which the observation and coaching occurs. Reflections from peer coaches reveal how fragile the coaching process is and highlight the need to understand and carefully consider the characteristics of growth-oriented feedback. Feedback provides "another set of eyes" to the teacher, affording another perspective on the teacher's work. It should be timely, specific, nonjudgmental, nonevaluative, directed toward behavior that can be changed, reciprocal, and meaningful. The effect of coaching can be magnified by the culture in which it occurs. This contextual factor is one of the essential ingredients addressed in Chapter 8.

Reflective Questions

1. What insights do you have as a result of reading this chapter?

2. Experiment with developing questions for the post-conference based on the goals for conferencing. Review your questions. Do they invite reflection, analysis, and the formulation of new ideas?

3. After examining the section on feedback, which are the most essential components from your perspective? How might they enhance the quality of coaching?

4. What do you predict will be the characteristics of a culture where coaching thrives?

8

Cultivating the Context for Peer Coaching

If you want to go quickly, go alone; if you want to go far, go together.

—African proverb

The organizational context in which coaching is implemented has a profound effect on how coaching is regarded, the level of risk taking and experimentation that faculty members are willing to commit to, the attitudes toward professional growth, the amount of collaboration among professional colleagues, and the results Peer Coaching produces in terms of staff and student learning. In turn, the positive presence of Peer Coaching affects the culture and climate of the school.

Six Conditions for a Peer Coaching Program to Flourish

For Peer Coaching to flourish, these six conditions must be in place:

1. There must be a *shared vision* of the Peer Coaching program, shaped by teacher input in response to the question "Why do this?"

2. There must be an environment that is hospitable to Peer Coaching; the *school culture* must be characterized by core values and beliefs that embrace interdependence and collaboration among teachers as the norm for interactions.

3. *Collegiality* must be embedded as a routine practice in daily work.

4. Relationships must be characterized by *trust* among professional colleagues.

5. The efforts of educators who consciously refine their practices so that every student thrives must be marked by regular *celebrations*.

6. There must be *support* for Peer Coaching in terms of time for professional learning, Peer Coaching activities, and follow-up; administrative endorsement and advocacy; and resources that align with Peer Coaching outcomes, including teacher autonomy to choose peer coaching structures and opportunities for purposeful play to build community, reduce stress, and promote creativity.

Preparing the Context with Questions as Guidance

Ray McNulty recently reflected that before schools commit to a change journey such as building and sustaining a Peer Coaching program, it is important to ask, "*Why* do we want to change? *What* do we want to change? *How* do we change?" (Personal communication, March 2014). Daniel Pink, in a recent interview with Amy M. Azzam (2014), noted, "We engage by getting someplace under our own steam" (p. 14). He pointed out that in order for adults [or students] to truly engage in an effort—that is, to really want to do it—"We have to increase the degree of autonomy people have over what they do; over how, when, and where they do it; and over whom they do it with" (p. 14). Individuals must have the opportunity to address the questions: "Why are we doing this in the first place? Why does it matter?" (p. 14). Answering the questions raised by McNulty and Pink provides direction for creating the context and conditions for Peer Coaching. For guidance, we must look to research and successful practice and, equally important, we must listen to the voices of teachers.

Why Do This? The Case for Collaboration

Why should we build collaborative work and formal coaching programs into our daily work in schools? The case for collaboration is compelling. DuFour (2011) notes, "There is abundant research linking higher levels of student achievement to educators who work in the collaborative culture of a professional learning community" (pp. 59–60). He cites John Hattie's 2009 work, *Visible Learning: A Synthesis of Over 800 Meta-Analyses Relating to Achievement,* as

> the most comprehensive study of factors affecting schooling ever conducted [in which Hattie] concluded that the most powerful strategy for helping students learn at higher levels was ensuring that teachers work collaboratively in teams to establish the essential learnings all students must acquire, to gather evidence of student learning through an ongoing assessment process, and to use the evidence of student learning to discuss, evaluate, plan, and improve their instruction. (DuFour; 2011, p. 60)

Certainly, Peer Coaching offers both collaborative and formal structures and processes to address these important ends.

Hargreaves and Fullan also emphasize that collaboration is key to improving schools for students and teachers. In their book *Professional Capital: Transforming Teaching in Every School* (2012), the authors address the critical roles that human and social capital play in sustained school improvement. Human capital refers to the qualities of individuals, such as a teacher's knowledge and skills. Social capital is the ability of groups to work collectively and effectively toward school improvement. It includes the relationships among professional colleagues that increase the collective capacity of staff to serve students, the school, or the system.

Emphasizing the need for collaborative work to capitalize on teachers' collective knowledge, given the multiple demands on teachers and the multiplicity of student needs, the president of the National Commission on Teaching and America's Future wrote the following:

> Quality teaching is not an individual accomplishment. It is the result of a collaborative culture that empowers teachers to team up to improve student learning beyond what any one of them can achieve alone.... The idea that a single teacher, working alone, can know and do everything to meet the diverse needs of 30

students every day throughout the school year has rarely worked, and it certainly won't meet the needs of learners in years to come. (Carroll, 2009, p. 13)

As these various citations suggest, the goals of Peer Coaching are very much aligned with what researchers and practitioners claim will be necessary for students, teachers, and schools to develop and prosper.

However, cultivating learning-focused collaborative cultures is easier said than done. We know that students' and staff members' opportunities to thrive increase when the context in which they learn is characterized by true collaboration. We also know that collaborative work among professional colleagues who enjoy trusting relationships increases the organizational capacity to solve problems; to amass internal resources to enhance instruction, curriculum, and assessment; and to increase teacher skillfulness and learning. Yet in many schools such collaboration is not the norm. Rather, there are norms that support privacy—going it alone. In addition, because individuals have historically worked in isolation in those settings, teachers often wonder, How do I measure up to the teacher on the other side of the classroom wall? The prospect of working collaboratively means that a teacher would have to expose her professional knowledge and skills publicly. Even if that individual would be willing to risk such professional exposure, multiple demands on time create additional challenges. In many settings, time has not been structured to create opportunities for collaboration. And even if the time structures have been established, teachers carefully weigh the potential benefits to be derived from collaborative endeavors in relation to the individual expectations for performance they face in their roles.

What Needs to Change?

To answer the question "*What* needs to change?" we must examine the culture of the school in which Peer Coaching will be embedded. To be able to construct, enhance, and sustain collaborative, learning-focused cultures where Peer Coaching can thrive, we must be able to identify attributes of school culture such as core values, norms, trust, risk taking, and use of time, all of which contribute to creating the organizational context needed for coaching to achieve coveted results. Additionally, it is important to examine how to transform those contexts with weak collaborative cultures or cultures of isolation. One leverage point for doing this is cultivating meaning. For educators to embrace Peer Coaching, the meaning and promise it holds must be greater than the cost of involvement.

Shared Vision: Creating Meaning for Every Member of the School Community

A peer coach once remarked, "Our faculties' shared vision for Peer Coaching and the shared vision for our school serve as a compass and help us focus our energies, chart our course, collect provisions for that journey, and stay the course." Shared vision is a purpose that can be witnessed in the daily activities of the school. Stephanie Hirsh (1995/1996), executive director of Learning Forward, describes vision as a descriptive statement of what the school will be like at a specified time in the future. The vision uses descriptive words or phrases and sometimes pictures to illustrate what one would expect to see, hear, and experience at a school at that time. It refers to the facility; the curriculum, instruction, and assessment; the staff; and the community. A shared vision galvanizes energies and motivates people. "The shared vision incorporates the hopes, dreams and aspirations of [organizational members]. When a vision is shared... it's easier to attract people, sustain a motivated workforce, and give people the energy and confidence to withstand hurdles and challenges on the road to building a successful company," explains Jim Kouzes (in Gallo, 2012) in an interview in which he reflected on the role of shared vision in business.

The process of creating a vision, which encourages faculty members to think about a school's purpose, may be as significant as the vision statement they ultimately develop. For a vision to come alive and guide people in their work, the development process must be participatory.

Involving faculty members brings both a sense of ownership and a commitment to the vision. The vision-development process gives people an opportunity to share their values and beliefs about schooling. These conversations build understanding, respect, and ultimately trust among professional colleagues. The shared vision then serves as a reference point for decisions about the focus of collaborative work and the resources devoted to its support, and it provides the *meaning* that drives participants' involvement in Peer Coaching. Having input into the direction of Peer Coaching by collaborating in the development of a shared vision provides faculty members with a sense of ownership and commitment to something that matters deeply to them. Emphasizing the importance of providing the opportunity for faculty members to influence the vision or direction of collaborative work, Daniel Pink (Azzam, 2014) emphatically states that schools need to "create an atmosphere in which people have a sufficient degree of freedom; can move toward mastery on something that matters; and know *why* they're doing something, not just how to do it" (p. 15). The atmosphere or climate in which Peer Coaching is to be implemented is dramatically influenced by school culture.

School Culture: The Stage on Which Coaching Plays Out

Although the classroom teacher is the single most powerful *school-based* influence on student achievement, school culture is the next most influential factor (Deal & Peterson, 2009; Marzano, 2003; Robbins & Alvy, 2014). The culture of the school can augment or diminish the resources available to classroom teachers. Bower states that, essentially, school culture is "the way we do things around here." Climate, on the other hand, is "how the workplace feels" (Deal & Peterson, 2009, pp. 5–7). Goleman, Boyatzis, and McKee (2002) explain, "When people feel good, they work at their best" (p. 14). Because the way people feel, interact, or do business on a daily basis at a school dramatically influences productivity for all its members, culture and climate are powerful school improvement tools. For example, at Parkside Middle

School in Prince William County, Virginia, the Leadership Team started a cultural tradition that influences interactions at every meeting. At the end of every meeting, a person is assigned to ask the following question: "What have we done or decided today to make the lives of Parkside students better?" This question permeates the fabric of daily life at the school and reminds organizational members of a core value of the school culture—making a positive difference in the life of each and every student.

Understanding the essence of culture helps those planning Peer Coaching programs to identify key leverage points. School culture has been defined as

> the practices that stem from a set of core values and beliefs influencing norms, interactions, operating procedures, reward structures, celebrations, physical environment, written and unwritten rules, expectations, perceptions, and relationships. Culture is steeped in history and tradition. It is carried on by organizational members who convey the essence of culture in their actions and interactions.... The culture of the school carries deep meaning for its members. It influences daily rituals and activities in the school—conversations, teaching practices, meetings, supervisory actions, hiring procedures, professional development, and student achievement. (Robbins & Alvy, 2014, p. 36)

Figure 8.1 (p. 113) shows key cultural leverage points for building or strengthening a Peer Coaching program. For example, every school culture has informal power brokers, or "priests and priestesses." These individuals have extraordinary influence over the thoughts and beliefs of their colleagues, who look to them for approval and guidance when asked to make decisions about topics that affect staff and students. Cultivating the priests' and priestesses' interest, understanding, and support of Peer Coaching is a strategic step in establishing or enhancing a program, because organizational members will look to these individuals for their advice.

FIGURE 8.1

Elements of Culture

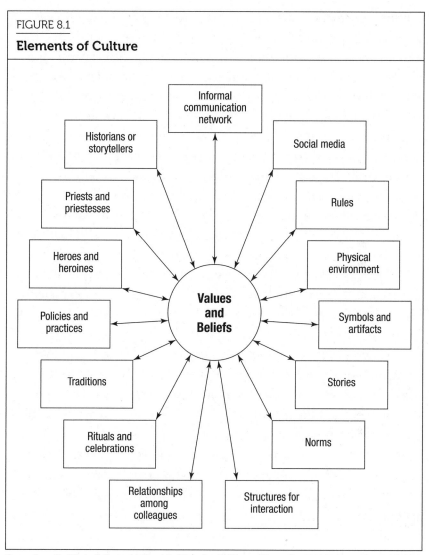

Source: From *The Principal's Companion* 4th ed. (p. 38), by Pam Robbins and Harvey Alvy, 2014. Thousand Oaks, CA: Corwin. Copyright © 2014 Corwin. Adapted by permission.

As indicated in Figure 8.1, another powerful leverage point for creating positive, collaborative, learning-focused professional communities is found in "structures for interaction." Developing structures to facilitate the sharing of successful practices—as well as mistakes,

reflective dialogue, student performance data, and problem solving—
is important work. Over time, members of the communities that form
and use these structures come to deeply value the rich expertise that
each person brings to the community. Together they take collective
responsibility for all students. As Kruse and Seashore-Louis (2009)
state, "The concept of *organizational learning* suggests that continuous
improvement through collective engagement with new ideas will
generate enhanced classroom practices and a deeper understanding of
how organizational improvement occurs" (p. 8). If schools have existing forums for collaboration such as data team meetings, lesson study
groups, faculty meetings, or grade-level or subject-area professional
learning communities, the presence of these structures will make the
implementation of Peer Coaching less daunting because pre-estab-
lished norms support collaborative efforts focused on the refinement
of practices to ensure student success. These collaborative experiences
also positively affect perceptions of job-embedded professional learning opportunities.

Dr. Kent Peterson (n.d.) notes, "School culture has a profound
effect on professional development. It affects attitudes toward spending time to improve instruction, motivation to attend professional
development and the [activities] people choose to participate in." If
structures for interaction are not in place within the culture of the
school, creating such structures provides avenues for professionals
to gather—face to face or electronically—to discuss topics of mutual
interest. These opportunities for learning-focused engagement and collaboration build endorsement and commitment over time. In addition,
organizational members find it energizing to see the results of their
collective endeavors.

Although the concept of culture is not new, what is new is that
specific cultural shifts have been found to have transformative power in
achieving results. Eaker and Keating (2008), for example, describe three
cultural shifts necessary for school cultures to function as professional
learning communities—a structure that, when implemented well, has
been documented to positively influence student achievement:

First, a shift in the fundamental purpose from teaching to learning. This shift is seismic. Second, a shift in the work of teachers... [T]eachers organize into high-performing, collaborative teams. Third, a shift in focus. Their focus shifts from inputs to outcomes and from intentions to results. (p. 15)

As illustrated in Chapters 2, 3, and 4, collaborative work activities and formal coaching structures reflect these three shifts. A peer coach offered this perspective regarding the shifts:

By emphasizing learning and results, our focus is on outcomes. This makes the act of coaching—no matter what the form—less threatening. We turn our attention to exploring what it is we do to derive desired results. In the process of examining our actions and the visible learning produced, we become better problem solvers and learn from one another too!

Another shift that radically changes life in the schoolhouse has to do with professional development. Donaldson's (2008) research demonstrated that supporting authentic learning in adults was positively linked to improving student achievement. However, Drago-Severson and Blum-DeStefano (2014) remind us that "because educators have different ways of knowing, they will need different supports and challenges in order to grow and improve their educational practice" (p. 29). So despite renewed interest in job-embedded learning as a way to provide sustained professional development within educators' daily routines rather than through isolated workshops or online course offerings, that learning must be differentiated to have the greatest effect. Embedding differentiated professional learning in daily coaching activities creates opportunities for teacher leadership, and it guarantees that the unique learning profiles and contexts of staff and students will be addressed. Participation in daily professional learning will generate greater motivation, endorsement, and engagement if the atmosphere seems safe and trust among professional colleagues has developed, producing collegiality.

From Isolation to Collegiality: Generating Energy and Momentum to Serve

Another important cultural shift is the one from norms of isolation to norms of collegiality. New norms of collegiality herald the collective knowledge and skills that can be amassed to serve students when adults in the schoolhouse voluntarily choose to come together, share craft knowledge, problem solve, plan, reflect on practice, and study what produces learning. However, to increase the desire for collegiality, it must be purposeful. To illustrate, in one high school that transitioned to the block schedule, it became apparent to staff members that students needed to engage in more physical movement within a 90-minute instructional period in order to remain engaged in rigorous tasks that required intense focus. "The students couldn't sustain efforts to remain on task without physical movement—but we wanted the movement to relate to our outcomes. We don't have any time to waste," one teacher stated. In response at a later faculty meeting, two physical education teachers presented and modeled transition techniques that involved physical movement but allowed students to remain focused on academic tasks. One example they modeled was a meet-and-greet transition with a silly handshake that required participants to exchange a note with a summary of what they had learned with the previous learning partner. Faculty members joined together to practice the techniques—many of which led to roars of laughter! After the presentation, the halls were abuzz with subject specific implementation ideas. This simple 10-minute experience began a tradition of collaborative work across disciplines focused on strategies to enhance teaching practices in ways that accelerated student learning. Over time, norms of collegiality developed, guided by a mutually held belief that "together we are richer than alone." Such sentiments thrive in an atmosphere characterized by trust among professional colleagues. Research and exemplary practice document that an essential ingredient of collegiality is trust.

Trust: A Building Block for Collaborative Work

Trust is a powerful building block for initiating and sustaining professional community and organizational learning. Bryk and Schneider (2004) and Tschannen-Moran (2004) suggest that trust among and between teachers and other groups is linked to increased student achievement. They explain that when professional colleagues perceive that trusting relationships exist, they are more likely to share successful practices and more willing to share problems of practice. They have less concern about being judged by other faculty members or being in competition with them.

Trust is developed by aligning actions with words, following through with commitments, keeping confidences, and modeling. The development of trust takes time and is enhanced by consistency. Trust among professional colleagues influences individuals' willingness to expose their knowledge or skills. When trust is low among colleagues, individuals are more comfortable participating in *low-risk* collaborative activities—those that don't require teachers to publicly demonstrate professional knowledge or skills. An example of a low-risk task might be an article review or a book talk, in which an individual would simply read, reflect, and engage in dialogue with colleagues. When trust is a bit greater, individuals might engage in *medium-risk* activities such as problem solving. A problem-solving forum would require an individual to demonstrate some knowledge or skill and expose beliefs, but would not require a stand-up performance in front of colleagues. If trust has been cultivated among professional colleagues, they tend to be willing to engage in *high-risk* activities such as coteaching or formal coaching. The provision of collaborative work activities as well as formal coaching structures allows organizational members to engage in activities that reflect their comfort levels, given the amount of trust in their relationships.

When individuals experience positive results and expanded resources as a result of working collaboratively, trust builds and the admiration of faculty members for the expertise that they "bring to the table" expands. In positive, collaborative, learning-focused contexts, learning is publicly celebrated, bringing buoyancy and renewed commitment to the work of the school.

Celebrations: A Call to What Matters

Ideally, celebrations reflect a school's core values and put them on display. They remind all stakeholders of what is important in the school. Celebrations add zest to the climate of the school and serve as motivators to organizational members—if they have meaning. It can be useful to make a list of a school's celebrations to examine if they reflect the core values of the culture and to assess if any values are not celebrated that should be. When faculty members collaborate in designing celebrations and regularly scheduling them, it focuses them on what matters. For example, at a back-to-school faculty meeting, tables of participants were asked to add up their collective years of experience in teaching; then the totals of each table group were tallied. When the faculty total was announced, it showed that the faculty represented thousands of years of wisdom! Reflecting on this notion and how it related to Peer Coaching, a teacher leader said, "When a teacher retires, a library of knowledge burns *if* we don't take time to learn from one another. This year, the Peer Coaching program will give us a menu of options from which to choose so that we can capitalize on and learn from the otherwise well-kept secrets about what makes a difference in every classroom. Here's to celebrating us!" Sparkling cider was passed and the faculty toasted to a successful year.

Celebrations in some schools have become a tradition. One school has a tradition called "See them teach before they leave." When a teacher is about to retire, that teacher invites all faculty members into the classroom either to watch her practice the craft of teaching or to converse about teaching and learning. The principal provides substitutes to release staff members to observe or personally substitutes in classrooms when there is a shortage of substitutes. Then, on the last day of school, a celebration is held. Staff members gather to honor the retiring teacher, who is presented with the doorknob from her classroom mounted on a plaque. The engraving reads, "Thank you for opening your door and sharing your expertise. You saved a library of knowledge from burning!" Another school has celebrations of teacher teams when students in a subject or grade level have demonstrated significant progress. Regardless of how a celebration is rolled out, what is celebrated should reflect what matters to staff and serve as a beacon, shedding light on treasured outcomes.

Celebrations offer one type of support for Peer Coaching by putting its goals and outcomes on display. The next section explores additional forms of support that contribute to the successful implementation of coaching.

Support for Peer Coaching: Many Forms and Many Places

Principals play a vital role in determining the success or failure of Peer Coaching. For coaching to succeed, principals must demonstrate their support in words and deeds, and they must genuinely value and believe in it. This belief in coaching is manifested in the way human, material, technological, and financial resources are allocated; time is scheduled; schoolwide norms of collaboration and risk taking are promoted; and professional learning occurs. Principals make time to talk about the importance of coaching to parents, students, school board members, staff, and central office personnel to generate understanding and support for the program. Where coaching is deeply valued, it has a prominent place in home-school publications, reports to the central office, weekly newsletters to the staff, and e-blasts. When Peer Coaching is on a faculty meeting agenda, it has a place at the top of an agenda, not at the bottom. During this "prime time," teachers are encouraged to participate in low- or medium-risk coaching activities that build their repertoire of skills to promote student learning or examine performance data and develop intervention plans. Principals who value Peer Coaching also serve as its champion by creating celebrations, sheltering those who engage in coaching from outside interference, and generating positive public relations about the program.

Principals who were asked about what motivated them to initiate, endorse, or support a Peer Coaching program responded with these comments:

> Feedback is the breakfast of champions! I cannot possibly get around to every member of the faculty as frequently as I would like. I believe that coaching gives staff members the opportunity to maximize the feedback available to them about teaching and learning.

> Every faculty member has the right to grow professionally. And I believe that professional growth should be differentiated with respect to the teacher's learning preferences, teaching style, personality, and perceived needs for professional learning. Peer Coaching provides a spectrum of options for addressing the "what" and "how" of professional development. By investing in teachers, we let them know we value them and we empower them to serve the diverse needs of an ever-changing student population.

> Teachers are overwhelmed with initiatives like Common Core; STEM; STEAM; new textbook adoptions; an iPad program... the list goes on. This is an incredibly busy place, and the pace has never been swifter. At the same time, kids are coming to our school with complex learning challenges in some cases, and needs for acceleration in others. Teachers cannot be expected to shoulder the burden alone. Peer Coaching provides a nonjudgmental source for on-the-job learning and a resource bank informed by other professionals to meet the unique demands they encounter daily. We owe them this support!

> Supporting educator growth is critical to student learning. We have a new teacher evaluation system that we are implementing here, among other things! But simply evaluating a teacher will not help him grow. I believe we have a moral and ethical obligation to provide job-embedded learning opportunities so that teachers can grow professionally and serve their colleagues and

our students. There is a sense of urgency about building human capacity to meet the new demands of practice. Doing this in a collaborative, learning-focused way is essential.

Regardless of the reasons that motivate principals to support Peer Coaching, a common thread runs through every program. Teachers sense the support and endorsement and are motivated to participate in Peer Coaching because of it.

Another critical component of support is the allocation of time. Time is a precious and scarce commodity in schools. Dedicating time in the daily or weekly schedule for coaching sends a powerful non-verbal message that coaching is important. Developing, implementing, and sustaining Peer Coaching will require time for orientation and planning, time for professional development, time for coaching activities—both collaborative work and formal coaching—and time to assess the program and make modifications as necessary. Teachers from schools that have successfully implemented Peer Coaching recommend that, whenever possible, Peer Coaching activities should be integrated into existing structures of learning-focused collaborative work. For instance, some schools have grade-level or subject-area professional learning communities or teams that meet regularly to discuss initiatives, student performance data, student work, curriculum, instruction, or assessment. Some of the collaborative work structures discussed in Chapter 3 may fit nicely with these existing structures.

Creating opportunities for teacher autonomy is another vibrant avenue of support. Freedom to choose is a powerful motivator for participation. Collaborative work structures and formal coaching activities offer several options from which teachers can choose. Daniel Pink advises, "Let's trust people with autonomy instead of assuming they can't handle it" (Azzam, 2014, p. 14). When individuals have the opportunity to select the focus of the work they wish to do, how they wish to work, and with whom, their engagement intensifies. As a consequence, the freedom to learn also creates an invitation for individuals to reflect on why they have chosen a specific focus. Talking about purpose—what matters—actually has been shown to enhance performance! (Pink, in Azzam, 2014, pp. 12–17).

Creating time for purposeful play can develop support for treasured Peer Coaching outcomes. For example, to highlight the importance of precision in language, coaching partners sit facing one another. One partner has a picture and the other partner, who cannot see the image, has a pen and paper. The person with the picture describes it with specificity so that the colleague can sketch it. Many times the result is amusing because the sketcher misinterprets the message that has been communicated. The person with the picture must provide helpful feedback without critiquing the sketcher's work. This activity often culminates with a deeper understanding of descriptive language and the process of giving feedback in formal coaching.

Brain research reveals that when we are more relaxed, learning actually becomes easier, innovative thinking increases, people see connections between seemingly disparate thoughts or entities, and they come up with new ideas. Scientists often remark that discoveries were made when people engaged in purposeful play. Pink notes, "Rigor and playfulness pair much more smoothly than we think they do—and pairing can have some pretty spectacular results!" (Azzam, 2014, p. 16).

Developing a context characterized by a shared sense of purpose and direction, unwavering support, trust, collaboration, time for interaction and experimentation, celebration of what matters, and opportunities to engage in meaningful work creates the space for teachers to reflect, analyze, make mistakes, learn, and experience the synergy that grows from working with others. These are the conditions that allow the work of peer coaches to succeed.

Summary

Peer Coaching programs are most likely to succeed in the presence of six conditions: shared vision; school culture characterized by values and beliefs that embrace interdependence and collaboration as the norm; trust among professional colleagues; collegiality embedded in the daily routine; regular celebrations; and support. Various questions may serve as guideposts for the Peer Coaching journey: Why change? What do we want to change? How can we change? Answers to these questions can come from research, exemplary practices, and from teachers and principals who have successfully engaged in the process. Chapter 9 will explore how to implement a Peer Coaching program so that it will ultimately become institutionalized within a learning community.

Reflective Questions

1. Which of the six conditions do you believe have the greatest influence in preparing the context for a Peer Coaching program?

2. As you reflect upon the three questions raised by Ray McNulty—Why change? What do we want to change? How to change?—how might they guide your efforts to develop or enhance a Peer Coaching program?

3. What did you think about Daniel Pink's discussion of engagement? Autonomy? Play?

4. Considering the context of the school in which you work, which of the conditions addressed in this chapter are in place and which may need additional cultivation?

9

Guiding the Implementation of a Peer Coaching Program

Why do this? To increase collaboration and conversation to improve teaching and learning.

—A 25-year veteran teacher from Michigan

As your school embarks upon or continues its Peer Coaching journey, this chapter can serve as a guidebook for your travels. Perhaps your staff has already addressed the question "Why do this?" and answered the question that follows, "What do we want to change?" We now turn our attention to "How do we change?"

The Three Phases of the Change Process

Studies of effective change efforts suggest that organizations that successfully institutionalize an innovation move through predictable phases. The classic RAND study "set out to characterize the process by which an innovation is translated into an operating reality within school districts" (Berman & McLaughlin, 1978, p. 13). The study revealed that "... three characteristic phases could be discerned within the overall process... mobilization, implementation, and institutionalization" (p. 13). Decades later, curriculum, instruction, assessment, the use of technology, and structures for interaction have evolved and changed in keeping with current trends, research, and practice. Despite advances in each of these areas, however, the phases of the change process in which they are employed remain constant and still serve as a useful framework for planning, implementing, and maintaining a Peer Coaching program.

The Mobilization Phase

The mobilization phase involves forming committees and creating awareness of what Peer Coaching is, how it works, and how it can support the work of teachers. Readiness activities are developed, scheduled, and presented. Planning begins, including the allocation of human, material, and financial resources. Ownership and commitment begin to emerge. This phase may last six months to an entire school year. The following paragraphs describe typical activities in this phase.

Forming a planning committee and developing a plan. To generate broad-based support for Peer Coaching, invite the entire staff to participate on the planning committee. Encourage individuals who have informal power and influence in the school culture to become committee members. Be sure to include representatives from the teachers association or union as members. Their involvement is key and can help dispel any myths that may emerge regarding Peer Coaching and evaluation. The planning committee's major functions are the following:

• Research Peer Coaching literature and programs.

• Identify Peer Coaching websites or videos, as well as school sites where Peer Coaching is in place and working effectively.

• Examine the context in which Peer Coaching is to be implemented to determine forces that would support or deter its implementation.

• Plan and present an awareness presentation for staff.

• Develop a program plan that includes differentiated coaching options (collaborative work and formal coaching) to present to the staff and garner their input and necessary revisions.

• Organize initial Peer Coaching activities once the staff has committed to a differentiated coaching plan.

This committee sometimes nominates an individual to handle the technical details of coaching, such as scheduling substitutes, developing conferencing and observation schedules, finding space for meetings, making sure technology works for observations, and making sure ready-made observation instruments are available, if desired.

Providing information about Peer Coaching. In the early stages of a change effort, people want to know what the proposed change is, what it looks like, and how it will affect them personally. To respond to these queries, it is important to define Peer Coaching, explain that it has nothing to do with evaluation, share the rationale for coaching, and provide examples of the different forms it can take. Here are some ways to provide initial information:

- Share articles about coaching.
- Arrange visits to schools where Peer Coaching has been successfully implemented.
- Create opportunities for staff members to shadow peer coaches.
- Share websites or videos that model Peer Coaching.
- Invite Peer Coaches to speak at PLC or faculty meetings.

A formal orientation session can be helpful. Ask teachers to generate questions they have about coaching and e-mail or send them to a teacher leader, principal, or assistant principal who is developing support for Peer Coaching. Then use the collective questions to structure the agenda. Schedule the orientation session at a convenient time for staff (hopefully with snacks and beverages provided), or develop an online orientation that can be accessed on demand. Provide tangible examples of how Peer Coaching works, and model adult-learning principles and collaborative work in the presentations. Start a blog about Peer Coaching following the orientation session to continue the conversations.

Developing a shared vision and purpose around coaching. Meaningful and responsive program planning must emanate from a clear understanding by staff members of what they envision the Peer Coaching program to look like, sound like, and feel like. Ultimately, staff input shapes the development of the shared vision as well as the purpose of the Peer Coaching program. Participating in the creation of the shared vision and the formulation of a purpose statement builds both a deeper understanding of coaching and a more intensified commitment to its desired ends. This process usually surfaces individuals' core values, and as a consequence, staff members often grow closer and more collegial. After developing a shared vision, they can construct goals to help bring that vision to reality, delineate activities aligned with those goals, and formulate benchmarks of progress that will allow staff members to reflect upon and assess their daily collaborative work in relation to the stated goals of the program. Activities such as these provide staff members with a way to connect with one another as resources, as problem solvers, or as fellow travelers on the Peer Coaching journey. Staff motivation springs from this type of involvement, and eventually coaching becomes an integral facet of the school culture.

Scheduling time. Time is an essential resource for Peer Coaching, and allocating time for coaching demonstrates support. Invite staff members to work together to identify where structured time for collaborative work currently exists and to determine whether Peer Coaching work could be integrated. An ever-present concern is whether time spent on coaching activities outweighs the value of time that would otherwise be used for individual teachers' routine responsibilities. Time for professional learning about Peer Coaching should be scheduled during prime time whenever possible.

When budgets are tight or it is difficult to secure substitute time due to personnel shortages, teachers, principals, and assistant principals have created opportunities for coaching in unique ways. In some cases, one teacher teaches her class and the class of a colleague in order to free that colleague to conference with and observe a third colleague. In other contexts, specialists have taken over classes to free teachers to conference with and observe their colleagues. Often principals and assistant principals have offered to function as substitutes to free up teachers to engage in Peer Coaching. When this happens, an added benefit is that students see administrators as facilitators of learning rather than in their traditional roles. Also, administrators gain a greater sense of the classroom realities that teachers face. Some teachers save time by using digital cameras or other devices to record themselves teaching and then simply meet with a colleague before or after school, or during a planning period to reflect upon and analyze the lesson.

Be aware that some of these methods of creating time can also drain energy over time and actually reduce the prospects for Peer Coaching success. How time is created for collaborative work and formal coaching should reflect the shared vision for the program and the unique characteristics of the school. When teachers can engage in collaborative work and formal coaching and gain new insights, refine teaching practices, analyze students' work, and watch student learning soar, they come to wholeheartedly embrace the coaching process and see it as an important and viable dimension of their professional role and a needed staple in the workplace.

Encouraging storytelling. One way to keep Peer Coaching in the fore-front of organizational members' eyes is through storytelling. During the mobilization phase, and throughout the implementation and maintenance phases, invite individuals to share coaching experiences with colleagues, as long as doing so doesn't infringe upon confidentiality. These offerings can be stories, testimonials, or sound bites. Sharing experiences can raise awareness within the culture of the school about how teachers are using coaching to examine and refine their practices to foster student learning, as well as influence the coaching work of others. Sometimes stories provide a note of levity. For example, a 1st grade teacher told the story of being in another 1st grade class for an observation. The focus of the visit was on the level of student engagement in relation to the teaching strategies used throughout the lesson. At the end of the lesson, a couple of students came up to the observer and said, "You ought to come back more often. We ain't ever been this good!"

Science teacher Holly Hilberg, from Sewickley Academy related her story of involvement with Peer Coaching as follows:

> The teachers in the triad I worked with had constructive conversations about our practices, and each of us received feedback

from another highly qualified professional. As we conferenced, observed, and debriefed with one another, we were challenged to clarify our intentions about our instruction. This affirms and celebrates what we do well and challenges us to analyze our choices and decisions in lesson design. Just as we like our students to learn at high levels—synthesis, analysis, and self-reflection—this model is structured so we can engage in critical thinking and analysis of our own practice. I knew I would learn through watching my peers; I didn't know I would learn about my own practice as my colleagues caused me to reflect upon my strengths. This raised my awareness of what I was doing. It is so important to have feedback and to listen to the ideas of others. I relish the notion of students observing us as we work together in teams. This is exactly what we expect our students to do! This modeling is so powerful!!

Another variation of storytelling involves case studies. One group of teachers new to coaching didn't feel comfortable inviting a colleague in to observe, but they wanted to work together. They decided to write case studies of classroom dilemmas—problems with which they were wrestling. When they had completed the case studies, the teachers organized in triads. They read one case study at a time, asked clarifying questions, and proposed interventions. After the meeting, they tried the proposed interventions in their classrooms and reported back to their colleagues. This activity went on for several months. Gradually, their trust in and respect for one another grew as a consequence of the collegial work. Eventually they began observing one another in classrooms. This example reminds us of the need to move slowly, taking time to build support, understanding, and trust.

Offering multiple Peer Coaching structures. Because teachers differ in their preferences for collaboration, efficacy, perceptions toward professional learning, and the trust they have in their colleagues, it is important to offer a menu of options for collaborative work and formal coaching, as discussed in Chapter 3. Providing specific examples of each option helps develop familiarity and comfort with the approaches. For example, illustrate how someone could become an action researcher in the classroom and investigate something that intrigues or puzzles the teacher—something meaningful. Discuss different interaction options as well as structures: pairs, triads, teams, grade levels, subject areas, or departments. Exploring these options will enable each faculty member to find the structure that represents the best fit at the time, recognizing that Peer Coaching is meant to evolve with the professional as needs and comfort levels dictate.

Planning how Peer Coaching will become institutionalized. A program becomes "institutionalized" when it becomes an integral part of the way business is conducted at a school. It becomes part of the fabric of the culture, influencing the daily activities of staff in the schoolhouse. New faculty members are acculturated to what was once the innovation and is now the norm. Successful change agents often remark that when change fails, it is because planning for institutionalization was neglected in the mobilization phase. They emphasize, for instance, the importance of taking time to talk about how Peer Coaching will be sustained and will evolve to meet the changing needs of staff over time. Thinking about how you want Peer Coaching to look when it is an integral part of the school can shed light upon important implementation-phase activities that you will embark upon to help reach that goal.

The Implementation Phase

Following the awareness-building and readiness-building activities of the mobilization phase, staff members will likely display greater commitment to collaborative work and formal coaching. By this time, resource allocations reflect a valuing of the program, and administrative support is explicit. It is during this implementation phase that professional learning opportunities are scheduled and conducted, follow-up activities occur, individuals have ample opportunities to practice collaborative work and formal coaching, celebrations of coaching experiences are held to recognize success and boost morale, feedback about coaching is generated, and modifications are made where indicated. It should be emphasized that participation in Peer Coaching needs to be voluntary, if possible. Early implementers will spread the word about its benefits, and interest and participation in coaching will expand as a consequence.

Professional learning sessions. When scheduling professional learning sessions, choose thoughtful intervals so that participants are not overwhelmed by the content or the processes, and so that they have an opportunity to practice applying the session's content. The design for the sessions should reflect principles of adult learning. For example, sessions should be goal oriented, practical and relevant to teachers' workplace realities, exemplify respect for their classroom responsibilities, and allow them to be self-directed and self-motivated. The presentation should include theory or research, demonstration or modeling, practice with feedback, reflection, and planning for application. Every session should be characterized by active learning. In some cases, training can take a flipped approach, with participants being asked to view a video, complete a reading, or engage in hands-on practice before a session. Handouts for every session should be available in both electronic and paper form to allow for the learning preferences of participants. The area in which the sessions occur should be large enough to accommodate participants sitting at table groups of four to six, allow for movement for collaborative work, and accommodate either stand-alone paper charts or wall space to post large sheets of paper for recording the brainstorming from each group. In addition, the room should be large enough to accommodate participant pairs and trios, as they engage in practice tasks and share their interactions with colleagues throughout the room. Reflection is an important part of every professional learning session. Some participants enjoy keeping electronic journals; others may record activities via blogs and Twitter posts, which remain available as part of the Peer Coaching effort. Appendix C presents examples of professional learning topics that may be addressed in sessions over time. The Student Learning Nexus (p. 83) can provide additional topics for professional learning sessions.

Before conducting pre-conferences, observations, and post-conferences in the classroom, it is helpful to conduct simulations in a training room context. To do so, form groups of six. One teacher functions as teacher (prepared with an adult-learning topic to teach, such as opening or closing activities, critical thinking skills, or integrating technology), three teachers serve as students, one teacher assumes the role of coach, and the remaining teacher functions as the coach's coach. The coach's coach helps formulate conferencing questions, talks through possible responses to the teacher, and verbalizes questions that may be helpful to both the coach and the teacher. For example, the coach's coach might say, "Try asking a question rather than making a statement. Notice how the teacher responds." The coach's coach speaks so that both the coach and the teacher can hear, since this is meant to be a learning experience. Rotate the roles so that every teacher has the opportunity to experience each role. Discuss the role-playing experience and the implications for classroom practice.

Schedule time for peer coaches to practice. For many teachers, the formal coaching experience is new and complex. Create opportunities for teachers to practice. In one school, teachers formed triads. Every teacher in each of the triads had the opportunity to participate in conducting two pre-conferences, two observations, and two post-conferences. In addition, each teacher participated in a pre-conference, was observed, and engaged in a post-conference with two colleagues. The schedule, artfully created by Cindy Bevevino, Sewickley Academy, Pennsylvania, provided for the following components:

- 20-minute pre-conference
- 20-minute observation
- 20-minute post-conference
- 10-minute reflection and debriefing

Teachers gained confidence in themselves as coaches and teachers as a result of this practice, as evidenced by the following reflections:

The practice we had was so helpful!

Wow! I looked at students in the observation applying the concepts of what we had learned about Visible Learning. It changed the way I saw the lesson!

I've struggled with avoiding judgments like "great lesson," but I have learned that substituting a description of teacher behavior and student consequences is so much more useful, and even more affirming to my colleague.

Provide follow-up support for professional learning. Plan both formal and informal ways for teachers to receive feedback about their efforts to implement concepts and strategies addressed during professional learning. This effort should include the coaching of coaches as they initially practice this role. Typically new coaches find it challenging to formulate questions, avoid judgmental language (such as "Awesome lesson!"), ask questions about observation data that foster metacognition, and collect data while observing the students as well as the teacher. In one school, the author shadowed the Peer Coaching process and intervened, with the teacher's and coach's permission, in the pre- and post-conferences as needed. In another setting, peer coaches recorded themselves conferencing and then reviewed and analyzed their work with colleagues. In still another context, coaches Skyped with the author.

Follow-up support can also include review and refinement sessions in which Peer Coaching participants have the opportunity to refine their teaching skills and coaching practices. In the process, teachers come together, share their work, problem solve, and express a need for additional instructional, curricular, assessment, or management strategies. "The most successful professional development efforts are those that provide regular opportunities for participants to share perspectives and seek solutions to common problems in an atmosphere of collegiality and professional respect" (Fullan, Bennett, & Rolheiser-Bennett, 1989; Little, 1982, cited in Guskey, 1995). Sessions can be face-to-face or online. In many cases, these sessions have led to follow-up learning opportunities. In one school, coaches expressed interest in a session entitled "How the Brain Learns: Implications for Teaching and Learning," which explored how the mind processes information and the implications for organizing and delivering curriculum, as well as instructional and assessment approaches. The skills that were taught, modeled, and practiced within the session were immediately applicable to the classroom. Peer Coaching participants invited colleagues who were not participating in coaching activities to this session. They also organized follow-up talks, bringing lessons they had developed and taught based on the workshop's principles, as well as the student work these lessons produced. Together, the participants analyzed the brain-compatible lessons and the student work; they then generated ideas for instructional next steps.

In a Colorado school, peer coaches became interested in the book *Classroom Instruction That Works: Research-Based Strategies for Increasing Student Achievement* (Dean, Hubbell, Pitler, & Stone, 2012). They created a book-study group and invited all staff members to attend, regardless of whether they were formally participating in coaching. They coplanned lessons based on the content of the chapters and engaged in formal coaching. Over time, these follow-up activities increased trust among professional colleagues, provided a common language, and enhanced collegiality.

Create ways to integrate coaching activities with other collaborative structures operating in the school. Work with planning committee members or other members of the school community to explore how coaching activities can be integrated into existing collaborative structures and functions. For example, one school began using collaborative work structures in PLC meetings and data team meetings. These actions bring important resources to learning-focused structures and simultaneously embed Peer Coaching in the culture of the school. The context of the school has a powerful and dynamic effect on implementation success. When Peer Coaching activities are integrated with existing structures, values, and processes, the potential for Peer Coaching to become a viable part of school culture increases tremendously. Further, integrating coaching helps staff members experience less fragmentation and perceive connections among what otherwise might be thought of as disparate innovations.

Construct a public forum for celebrating Peer Coaching successes. Research tells us that halfway through a change effort a condition called *entropy*, or "running out of steam," commonly surfaces. In other words, change efforts often lose momentum during this period. To counteract this phenomenon, it is important to revisit the history of Peer Coaching efforts at the school, celebrate progress, and recognize successes (without compromising agreements of confidentiality). This effort often involves inviting testimonials, such as this one from a teacher:

> I used to lock people out of my classroom and post paper on the window of the door. Now that I have been participating in Peer Coaching for seven months, I welcome another set of eyes in my classroom. My coach's questioning strategies, as well as the opportunity to watch him teach, have made a significant difference in the performance of my students!

Celebrations energize the staff and breathe vitality into the Peer Coaching effort. They might occur within a faculty meeting, a school board meeting, or a PTO-faculty recognition meeting. Some schools use local media to celebrate positive teacher initiatives. Many post their celebrations on the school's Facebook page.

The Institutionalization Phase

As Peer Coaching is implemented and sustained over time, the ultimate goal is its seamless integration into the school culture. Hence, when Peer Coaching becomes institutionalized, it will no longer be an innovation but an integral part of the school itself. To become institutionalized, Peer Coaching practices must adapt to the unique context variables of the school and its staff. Highlighting the importance of doing this, Guskey (1995) describes the teaching and learning process as "a complex endeavor that is embedded in contexts that are highly diverse" (p. 2). He adds that innovations in education today succeed "to the degree that they adapt to and capitalize on this variability… Contexts involve organizations which must develop along with the individuals within them" (p. 2).

Miles and Louis (1987) offer the following "signposts of success" as indicators of institutionalization:

- The change is accepted by relevant actors.
- Implementation is stable and routine.
- The change is widely used.
- Continuation is expected and usually accompanied by negotiated agreements.
- The change has achieved legitimacy and normality; it is no longer seen as a change but has become invisible and is taken for granted.
- The change is person-independent; continuation does not depend on the actions of specific individuals, but on organizational structure, procedures, or culture.
- Allocations of time and money are routinely made.

To achieve institutionalization status, the organization's members must perceive Peer Coaching activities as meaningful, useful, and worth continuing. Its processes must become embedded in the way school business is conducted: how the school solves problems, shares in decision making, promotes teacher leadership, and applauds individual initiatives. Institutionalization is perhaps the most difficult of the three phases to accomplish. The following paragraphs describe ways to keep the momentum going.

Regularly evaluate Peer Coaching activities to determine if midcourse adjustments are necessary. Doing so will ensure that the collaborative work is aligned with the perceived needs of the staff as well as the organizational demands related to focus, such as CCSS or state standards. Include relevant groups, representative of the entire school, when asking for feedback so that the evaluation data reflect the views of members of the entire organization. Ask questions such as these:

- Is Peer Coaching on the right track?
- Have there been challenges in implementing Peer Coaching?
- Do Peer Coaching activities build the knowledge base and skillfulness of individual teachers? If so, in what ways? If not, why not?
- Are the structures for collaborative work functioning to increase the problem-solving capacity of those who use them? If so, how? If not, why not?

- Have collaborative work structures become meaningfully integrated with existing forums for joint work focused on school improvement, staff, and student learning? If so, how? If not, why not?
- Does the implementation of Peer Coaching practices positively affect student learning? If so, in what ways? If not, why not?

Answers to questions such as these help program planners monitor and adjust Peer Coaching so that it is responsive and able to serve members of the school's culture. Research on the change process underscores the need for innovations to skillfully address context variables if implementation is to succeed and lead to institutionalization.

Continue to monitor. Evaluation reflects data at one point in time. However, constantly examining qualitative data is essential to ensure that Peer Coaching remains on track. Examine the shared vision and goals. Are coaching activities addressing these? Are adjustments necessary? What is the focus of hallway conversations? Faculty forums?

Continue the celebrations. Create special events that celebrate Peer Coaching accomplishments on an ongoing basis. One school's faculty workroom is adorned with a "wall of knowledge" that depicts ideas, articles, research, quotes, books, websites, and data that manifest the collective knowledge base that builds the staff's capacity to enrich the learning experiences students have access to in classrooms. Every month, a "celebration of knowledge" at a faculty meeting highlights new additions to the wall.

Support teachers as researchers. Peer coaches constantly seek to address classroom dilemmas, and in doing so, they refine or enhance teaching practices that culminate in high levels of student learning. Creating shared planning time, allocating resources, and expanding opportunities to network are ways to offer teachers, as reflective practitioners, the opportunity to continue to grow.

Continue leadership support. Administrators and other school leaders, including teacher leaders, can use several tools to focus attention, convey importance, influence attitudes, and reinforce values toward Peer Coaching. Here are a few of those supports:

- Allocating financial resources for coaching activities.
- Modeling risk taking and experimentation.
- Spending time on Peer Coaching in meetings.
- Asking questions about Peer Coaching.
- Conducting Peer Coaching in special settings to convey its importance.
- Placing Peer Coaching information in e-mails, newsletters, blogs, daily bulletins, Twitter postings, and reports.
- Telling coaching-related stories and using metaphors to underscore the importance of Peer Coaching.
- Structuring the decision-making and problem-solving processes used in meetings to reflect Peer Coaching practices.
- Placing Peer Coaching prominently on faculty meeting agendas.
- Developing a slogan or logo with staff and students about Peer Coaching to keep it in the forefront of school life.
- Speaking about Peer Coaching with students, parents, central office staff, and the community at large.

Engage teachers new to the school in Peer Coaching orientation sessions. Create opportunities for new staff members to learn about Peer Coaching and participate in coaching activities. Some schools have integrated Peer Coaching and mentoring activities for new teachers. The goal is to make coaching activities inclusive as opposed to exclusive, and to provide support for collegial work that positively affects learning at all levels. A teacher new to a school offered the following comment:

> Peer Coaching made it OK, in fact communicated an expectation, that I should ask questions about teaching and learning. It was a great feeling to know that support was available just a few yards down the corridor! I didn't get this kind of support at my former school. I am here to stay!"

It is interesting to note that research confirms that working conditions have a positive effect on teacher retention in a school. "Studies show that one of the greatest incentives in teachers' choices of schools is the opportunity to work with other skillful and committed colleagues, and to be in environments where they can be efficacious" (Darling-Hammond, 2010, p. 208).

Encourage teachers to reflect and write about Peer Coaching. Teachers can add to the collective knowledge base about coaching practices by writing articles for professional journals and contributing to electronic logs and blogs. These written accounts spread the word about Peer Coaching and its effects to other professionals, increase participation, and provide intrinsic rewards and professional growth opportunities for teachers.

When Peer Coaching becomes a genuine part of school operations, schools maximize their capacity to address challenges. Teachers are empowered to make decisions about their work and have access to an expanded network of resources to address local, state, or federal mandates and to increase their capacity to serve an ever-changing population of diverse learners. They enjoy opportunities for participation and leadership in a collaborative, learning-focused workplace. Teachers have become responsible for the success of Peer Coaching. Coaching is no longer a superficial innovation tacked onto the school for another year; rather it is part of the school's inner workings—its soul, deep and enduring. When Peer Coaching becomes institutionalized, educators' lives change. As one teacher remarked, "Even for the most severe problems, there is colleagueship and, beyond that, companionship on this journey to make a difference. The support is ubiquitous. I am not alone anymore."

Summary

A successful Peer Coaching program can be developed using a framework with three phases: mobilization, implementation, and institutionalization. Each phase includes several critical steps to support the effort. The ultimate goal is to seamlessly integrate Peer Coaching practices so that they become a part of the way business is transacted at a school, contributing a reservoir of rich professional learning opportunities, accessible to all staff members to inform their work in teaching and learning.

The ideas presented in this chapter are not new or revolutionary. Some readers might even find them self-evident. Yet, as Guskey (1995) reminds us, "it is rare to find a professional development effort today that is designed and implemented with thorough attention to these… factors. It is rarer still to find professional learning endeavors that evaluate implementation in terms of effects on student learning" (p. 7).

When thoroughly implemented, Peer Coaching adds meaning and resources to teachers' work and their ability to respond to the ever-changing demands of their roles. Ultimately, it fuels professional growth, commitment, and refinement of teaching practices, and enhances student learning. The challenge? Keeping the momentum and the synergy alive, which is the focus of Chapter 10.

Reflective Questions

1. Thinking about the context in which you work, in which phase of the change process are staff members currently working?

2. What do you believe are the most critical activities in the mobilization phase? The implementation phase? The institutionalization phase?

3. In what ways do you see opportunities to integrate coaching practices with existing PLC work?

4. How do you think coaching strategies can be leveraged to enhance teacher skillfulness and enrich student learning?

10

Keeping the Momentum Going
for Peer Coaching Success

As our school changes and people come and go, there should be enough roots now for Peer Coaching to spread.

—Annellen Cooper Robertson
Math Department Chair, Parkside Middle School

Although Peer Coaching offers great potential—refined teaching practices, a broader resource bank from which to draw, improved student achievement—it also takes effort, focus, and time to maintain. Despite how much educators may embrace its value, maintaining momentum takes a lot of energy. Furthermore, competing variables for attention emerge over time. Although this can be viewed as an obstacle, if Peer Coaching is well integrated into a school's culture, it can morph into an avenue to address those variables. For instance, one district was facing pressure to adopt a new literacy initiative related to the implementation of Common Core standards. Because so many staff members had previous positive experiences with Peer Coaching, it soon became viewed as a viable and welcome structure to facilitate implementation of the initiative. Additionally, as new staff members join the school community, it's important that they be invited to become a part of the Peer Coaching program. Newcomers' insights, perspectives, and enthusiasm infuse energy and fervor into the Peer Coaching process. In addition, inviting newcomers into Peer Coaching creates a more inclusive culture.

Unlike many initiatives that are created reactively—in response to local, state, or federal mandates—Peer Coaching is, as described in this book, a program with several adaptable structures. Therefore, although mandates often draw resistance, usually that is not the case with Peer Coaching. However, even coaching efforts can run out of steam, as was discussed in Chapter 9 when we explored the concept of entropy. Demands on individuals' time, the labor and costs involved with orchestrating schedules to facilitate formal coaching, and creating time in the weekly schedule for professional dialogue all point to the precarious nature of building and maintaining the momentum for coaching. Understanding the complexities of the change process can help program planners navigate dilemmas, difficulties, and bumps in the road so that coaching can flourish. This chapter reveals the insights and cautions of researchers, intended to illuminate the murky change journey so that it will lead to desired results.

Understanding Change

Fullan (2007) reminds us that change is not neat, but rather messy most of the time. Change is not linear. For some, change brings a sense of loss—loss of familiar ways of doing things, established norms—triggering powerful individual or collective emotions. New ways of doing things often cause feelings of vulnerability because of the unknown. Some people interpret an invitation to do new things as an indication that what they had been doing was wrong. As these points illustrate, change often requires both a technical and an emotional response.

When Change Does Not Produce Immediate Results

Many change facilitators lose heart when immediate results do not occur as a consequence of a change effort. Rosabeth Moss Kantor (1997) offers a helpful insight with respect to the notion that if change doesn't immediately produce results, it is tempting to move on to the new best thing:

The difference between success and failure is often just a matter of time: staying with the project long enough to overcome the unexpected developments, political problems, or fatigue that can come between a great-sounding plan and actual results. A basic truth of management—if not of life—is that nearly everything looks like a failure in the middle. At the same time, of course, the next project always looks more attractive (because it is all promise, fresh, and untried). (p. 129)

Ironically, if the change process gets off to a smooth start, it may be an indication that something is wrong. The change may have been implemented too quickly. Or, in the beginning, staff members may be holding back their opposition and just going along with it. Phil Schlechty (2001) reminds us that "compared to sustaining change, starting change is relatively easy" (p. 39). He points out that this is why more changes are initiated in schools than are sustained. Writing about the challenge of sustaining change, he notes, "Two things sustain change: one is a leader or leadership group that acts as a change agent; the other is a system or group of systems that supports change" (p. 40). Therefore, if the school culture does not have the capacity to sustain a change effort, "the change rarely outlasts the tenure of the change agent" (p. 40). Thus it is important to study and then create those systemic conditions in the school culture that will support and sustain a change. For a change to succeed in the workplace, the change and the mind-set for change must take hold. Do not ask the administration if the change has occurred—visit classrooms. Then visit the classrooms two years later. Are there now coaches in school who can train new staff members? That is, has the change been institutionalized? All personnel should be learning together throughout the system. Changing what people in the organization value and how they work together to accomplish it leads to deep, lasting change in the culture of the school (Fullan, 2002).

The Holistic Nature of Change

"Because change is holistic, every aspect of the organizational system has the potential to be affected. This underscores the importance of systemic thinking; that is, that changes in one part of the system have an impact on others" (Robbins & Alvy, 2014, p. 97). For example, formal coaching affects teachers—both the teacher who will be observing and the inviting teacher. Using substitute teachers to release coaches affects the substitute pool, the principal who will have a substitute in the building, and the students who are in the class that the substitute will teach. Additionally, students will tell their parents that their teacher was replaced by a substitute for part of the school day. Being aware of the many systemic effects of a single activity allows you to be proactive in preparation.

Perceptions and Change

Michael Fullan once explained to a group of professional developers, "The proof is in the putting. How something is put forth in large part determines how it will be received." This quote has important implications for program planners and other school leaders. Thinking about those who will be affected by a change, as well as the change itself, helps one to shape the message about the change, as well as how it will be delivered. To build interest and meaning for individuals who would be affected by a change, the California School Leadership Academy in Hayward, California, identified four factors that can be used to facilitate change. When communicating about the change effort, the following factors should be considered:

- *Relevance*—how the change is relevant to one's work life or responsibilities.
- *Feasibility*—whether the change is "doable" given other demands on one's time, skills, and philosophical beliefs.
- *Involvement*—whether individuals affected by the change have input into what the change will look like, sound like, and feel like.

• *Trust*—whether there is trust between the individuals being asked to change and the facilitator or initiators of the change.

If faculty members have collaboratively created a shared vision about high-quality teaching and staff and student learning, and if a proposed change, Peer Coaching, is aligned with the shared vision, it is probable that the change will be heartily embraced. People will view it as *relevant*, they will perceive it as *feasible*, it will have meaning because of faculty members' prior *involvement* with developing the shared vision, and an atmosphere of *trust* will have been established in the process (adapted from Robbins & Alvy, 2014, pp. 104–105).

Responding to Concerns

Successful change facilitators pay attention to how individuals affected by a change express interest or concern. Reactions to change tend to develop in a fairly predictable way. According to research by Hord, Rutherford, Huling-Austin, and Hall (1987), when a change is introduced, faculty members initially want information about "What is it?" If change facilitators provide that data, concerns will then turn to "How will this change affect me?" Once an answer is provided, the next question that faculty will ponder is "How do I manage this?" Finally, once this question has been addressed, faculty members will ask, "What will be the impact of this change initiative?" Knowing how concerns evolve over time helps the change initiators and facilitators craft their responses to questions. Ironically, many change facilitators try to "sell" a change by talking about its benefits. Obviously, in the initial stages of the change process people are not concerned about benefits. They want to know more basic information about the change and how it will affect them.

Creating Commitment to Change

Phil Schlechty (1993) explains, "Creating commitment to change is not the same thing as overcoming resistance to change. To create

commitment, one must understand motives" (p. 50). Schlechty out-
lines five role-types and details what motivates each of them:

> *Trailblazers* are motivated by novelty, excitement, and sometimes
> the possibility of fame and glory. *Pioneers* sometimes begin their
> journey because of intolerable conditions, but they will stay the
> course only if they become convinced that the new world is really
> better. *Settlers* need to know, almost for certain, that the world
> they are being asked to move to is better than the one they are
> leaving and that the way to get there is known. And, most of all,
> they need to know they are not taking the trip alone. *Stay-at-
> homes* will only move when all—or nearly all—of their friends
> and neighbors have deserted them or when they muster the cour-
> age to "come for a visit" and find that they prefer it. Some *sabo-
> teurs* will never come along, and if they do, they will make the
> trip as difficult as possible. Saboteurs, however, are people who in
> some prior movement to another frontier, behaved as trailblazers
> and pioneers, but were betrayed by their leaders. As a result, they
> became cynical about the prospects of change. Most of all, they
> want to be assured that those who are sounding the latest call
> to move to a new frontier will stay the course rather than turn
> around and go back. (pp. 50–51)

For change leaders, understanding what motivates each of the role
types can be helpful in planning how to differentiate responses to each
of these players to build commitment and support. Schlechty's view
on the reason behind some cynicism toward change is a reminder of
the potential hazards of jumping on and off new bandwagons every
year and not continuing the journey to institutionalization. Hence
organizational members often proclaim, "If you wait just long enough,
this too will pass!" Although saboteurs are the most difficult players
to bring along on a change journey, some of their criticisms may offer
useful insights for sustaining responsive change.

Negative Feedback as a Catalyst for Positive Results

It is important to identify ways to request feedback throughout all phases of a change effort. Although negative feedback is difficult to receive, if it is embraced openly and examined carefully, it can illuminate areas of needed improvement and enhance implementation processes. Often negative feedback is perceived as an outright rejection of a change initiative. However, if those who generate negative feedback feel that their viewpoints are heard and perceive that their concerns can influence policy and practice for the better, they may even become partners and advocates of the change. At one school, parents expressed displeasure that their children's teachers were out of the classroom due to Peer Coaching activities twice a month. In response, the school organized an open house and invited parents to attend. During the open house, the goals of the Peer Coaching program were outlined and teachers gave examples of how lessons that resulted from collaborative work and formal coaching directly benefited the students. Then parents were invited to ask questions or voice concerns. Their input informed future coaching activities, which included regular updates to the school's Facebook page regarding the focus of Peer Coaching work.

Using Human Relations to Leverage Change

Organizations change as the people within them change. Having a toolbox of strategies to interact meaningfully with other members of the organization facilitates their willingness to adapt and commit to change. Commenting on the importance of relationships, Scott and McLain (2011) state the following:

> Relationships are at the heart of what we do ... relationship is our most valuable currency. If we don't connect with peoples' hearts as well as their heads, it's not likely we'll move forward collectively ... I believe we either build a bridge or a wall with every person we meet. (p. 61)

If the culture of a school is grounded in positive, trusting relationships among professional colleagues, then difficult conversations are commonplace. Learning how to disagree respectfully and listen to the perspectives of others without judgment empowers staff members with the ability to focus on the topic at hand. Focusing the conversation on the practice rather than the person diminishes the emotional impact of having one's ideas examined and increases the willingness to reflect and revise one's thinking.

Task and Relationship Behaviors

Human relations skills require that we simultaneously balance task and relationship behaviors. If too much emphasis is placed on task behaviors as a measure of success, faculty members may feel stressed or pressured. On the other hand, if too much emphasis is placed on relationship behaviors, people may feel "it's all fluff." Strategically, in the initial stages of creating a trusting Peer Coaching partnership, professional colleagues may focus on relationship behaviors and choose tasks that are low-risk. As trust builds and partners become more comfortable exposing vulnerabilities and experimenting with new teaching strategies, they gradually integrate more high-risk, task-oriented behaviors. Optimally, successful Peer Coaching requires a balance of task and relationship behaviors in order to sustain momentum and realize continuous results.

Promise and Possibility

As you reflect upon the ideas about change presented in this chapter, hopefully you have identified findings that will enrich the content and processes of efforts to build, sustain, or add momentum to your Peer Coaching work. Although the path to success may be riddled with obstacles and require great energy and commitment to traverse, the rewards of the Peer Coaching journey will be plentiful. The web of relationships that Peer Coaching creates within a school helps connect the minds and hearts of organizational members, generating synergy for continuous improvement and renewal. This synergy creates an internal capacity to build systemwide support to enhance professional practice and student learning. As teachers grow, learn, contribute ideas and insights, problem solve, invent new ways of doing things, and take on leadership roles, they shape classrooms and culture. Coaching can boost teacher effectiveness, enrich student learning, deepen subject-area understanding and expertise, and improve relationships among professional colleagues. Principals, assistant principals, and other school leaders demonstrate their support and endorsement with words and deeds. With a positive mindset and unwavering dedication, obstacles can be leveraged into opportunities. The journey, guided by the needs of students, in a climate and culture nurtured by caring adults, is infused with hope. Implementing Peer Coaching provides both promise and endless possibilities for the future of students and those who educate them.

Summary

Despite the value of Peer Coaching and its propensity to enrich professional practice, build a more learning-focused collaborative culture, and boost student learning, it is difficult to sustain over time. At the very least, keeping the momentum going is a constant challenge. To address these difficulties, researchers and practitioners have offered various insights and cautions that can inform the change journey.

Among their conclusions is the notion that change tends to be messy. It brings with it a sense of loss—loss of the familiar. It can create feelings of vulnerability—new conditions in the environment and a sense of self-doubt at times. Because of the emotional nature of these responses, addressing organizational members' concerns requires both a rational or technical, as well as an emotional, response. Rosabeth Moss Kantor's writings provide the insight that "the difference between success or failure [of a change initiative] is often just a matter of time... nearly everything looks like failure in the middle" (p. 129). Phil

Schlechty reminds us that compared to sustaining change, initiating it is relatively easy. His insights include the importance of preparing the culture in which the change is to be embedded, lest the change disappear when the change initiator leaves. Fullan's work offers the perspective that in order to realize deep, lasting change, we must change what people in the organization value and how they work together to accomplish it in the culture of the school.

The notion that change is holistic reminds us that changes in one part of the system influence other parts. Tailoring one's responses to the perceptions, concerns, and motives of organizational members can increase the positive effect that those responses may have and can help people to engage, overcome resistance, or ramp up their support for an initiative. Additionally, negative feedback can serve as a positive catalyst for change if it is embraced openly, with a stance of "what can we learn from this perspective?" Finally, human relations skills are essential as an empowering tool to build bridges. In conclusion, Peer Coaching offers a vision of hope—the promise and possibilities for system, staff, and student learning.

Reflective Questions

1. Thinking about change efforts with which you have been involved, which of the chapter's concepts resonated with you?

2. In what ways might sustaining change be more difficult than initiating it?

3. What are some ways to change what people value and how they work together to accomplish those ends in organizations?

4. From your perspective, what changes in the culture of a school are needed to successfully embed and sustain Peer Coaching?

5. What new insights do you have as a result of reading this book?

Appendix A:
Reflections from School Leaders

☞ Why Peer Coaching

Kolia O'Connor is Head of Sewickley Academy in Sewickley, Pa. O'Connor reflects on the benefits of peer coaching and shares why he and his school engage in peer coaching.

In a world seeking greater accountability of teachers, we know that supporting teachers to improve their classroom practice is critical if labor intensive. Some believe that only supervisory feedback can support teacher growth and learning, but this is both inaccurate and misguided. Where teachers are committed to their individual and collective professional growth (which means they are committed to improving their ability to support the children in their classrooms to achieve ever stronger outcomes), a culture exists where faculty, through a process of peer coaching, can support real improvement in the learning experiences of their students.

The fact is that there are never enough supervisors to provide the quality and quantity of feedback to allow classroom teachers to learn and grow over time. Schools have routinely found themselves creating schedules for faculty evaluation that mean that each member of faculty is evaluated once in a three- or four-year cycle. Such a framework, if it is the sole mechanism for providing feedback on classroom practice, is woefully inadequate to enhance a teacher's performance in the classroom.

Enter peer coaching. With training and guidance, teachers can—and should be able to—support one another in the achievement of specific learning outcomes relating to their work in the classroom. High-quality feedback does not need to be supervisory. In fact, it could be argued that, with the proper training, nonsupervisory feedback, because it is less threatening, might actually be of greater value. Peer coaching then becomes a useful tool for gathering data about practice that provides a teacher with the feedback necessary to inform reflection (What am I doing? What is its impact on the children I am teaching? How can I modify what I am doing to improve the experience and the outcomes for students in my classroom?).

Moreover, peer coaching supports the professional growth of both the observer and the observed. In such a framework, the observer reflects on what has been observed, on how those observations may yield valuable information that the teacher can use, and on how to communicate those observations in a way that will promote growth. The teacher, in turn, must reflect with sufficient rigor on her classroom practice so that she can ask for the guidance and feedback necessary to make adjustments and improve the work. Both participants are actively engaged in thinking about what constitutes good teaching, what that looks like in a particular context, and how the teacher can elicit the best performance possible from students. Further, schools benefit from the use of peer coaching for the way it helps to create and support a culture of shared commitment; a focus on the needs of children; and an environment that promotes professional, collegial conversation.

At Sewickley Academy, we feel that our students benefit from being in an environment where their teachers are also learners, honing their craft and deliberately trying to create the best possible experience for their students. Coaching enhances professional practice and the quality of learning experiences that students encounter by increasing the amount of feedback available to teachers about their instruction, the implementation of curriculum, and the various modes of assessment. Interdisciplinary and professional in focus, peer coaching becomes a significant professional development activity and creates opportunities for collaboration between and among various teachers. All this activity helps to inform and strengthen the professional, collegial, and student-focused community that characterizes the best schools.

⟜ One District's Experience with Peer Coaching

Dr. Renée Schuster is the former superintendent of the Community Consolidated School District 181 outside Chicago. In response to a series of questions, she described her district's experience with Peer Coaching.

How and why did you decide to get involved in Peer Coaching?

During the 2012–2013 school year, a task force in District 181 developed a plan, which would integrate the implementation of the Common Core standards with the district's curriculum renewal cycle, school improvement plans, and recommendations from a program evaluation of our gifted and talented program. This plan became known within District 181 as the Learning for All Plan. Based upon the research of Joyce and Showers and our own experiences, we realized that if we wanted to achieve high levels of implementation, our professional development would need to include coaching. The Learning for All Plan called for a professional development cycle that included coaching, as illustrated below.

Under this model, professional development began with an awareness session followed by direct instruction. The third step in the professional development cycle involved job-embedded coaching using the "gradual release of responsibility" process also called *I do, We do, You do*. Instead of having a substitute teacher cover the class while the teacher was away for professional development, the coach joined the teacher in class.

First, the coach implements the new curriculum, instructional practice, or assessment strategy while the teacher observes. This is the *I do (Model)* portion of the gradual release of responsibility process. After this lesson, the coach and teacher meet to discuss the lesson and answer any questions the teacher may have. Next, the coach and the teacher implement the new curriculum, instructional practice, or assessment strategy together, in the *We do (Supported Application)* part of gradual release, again followed by time to discuss the lesson and answer questions. The final step in the gradual release of responsibility process is for the teacher to implement and apply their new learning while the coach observes, also called the *You do (Application)* step in the *I do–We do–You do* process. After this lesson, the teacher and coach discuss the lesson and the coach provides feedback and answers any questions.

The Learning for All Plan also called for adding coaching positions and coaching responsibilities to several existing positions, including reading specialists, differentiation specialists (formerly called gifted specialists), media resource center (MRC) directors, and school psychologists. In 2012–2013, we added our first literacy coaching positions, which we shifted to instructional coaches in 2014–2015. Our Department of Learning researched different approaches to coaching and decided to focus our professional development on Peer Coaching because we wanted to create a culture of coaching built upon collaboration through which all staff learn together and share their expertise. In 2013–2014, we began Peer Coaching with a year of professional development in which teams from every school participated in monthly full-day sessions. The school teams included the reading specialist, differentiation specialist, MRC director, school psychologist, a classroom teacher, a special educator, and the principal. In addition, a representative from each instructional position was included in at least one building team (e.g., teacher assistant, speech-language pathologist, occupational therapist, social worker). District administrators coordinated and participated in the professional development.

How was your Peer Coaching program designed/structured?

Certain positions were designated as having coaching responsibilities as part of their positions. These included our instructional coaches, reading specialists, differentiation specialists, MRC directors, and school psychologists. We included our principals in the professional development so they could lead the improvement effort and use coaching techniques within the teacher and staff evaluation process.

Our Peer Coaching was built upon the premise of gradual release (I do, We do, You do), in which the coach would model the new curriculum, instructional strategy, or skill while the teacher observed; then the coach and teacher would implement the new curriculum, strategy, or skill together; and finally the teacher would implement while the coach observed.

Who participated in the program?

Every school formed a team to participate in the professional development, which included their reading specialist, differentiation specialist, MRC director, school psychologist, a classroom teacher, a special educator, and the principal. In addition, a representative from each instructional position was included in at least one building team (e.g., teacher assistant, speech-language pathologist, occupational therapist, social worker). District administrators coordinated and participated in the professional development.

One of the expectations from the professional development sessions was that each school team share their learning with all staff at the school, so at some level, all staff participated in the Peer Coaching program. The vision is for Peer Coaching to be a major component of professional development within District 181. Any staff member who is implementing new curriculum, assessments, or instructional strategies will participate in Peer Coaching as part of the professional development process.

What do you perceive were the outcomes of the Peer Coaching effort?

We perceived several outcomes from the implementation of Peer Coaching, including the following:

1. Increased conversation about improving teaching and learning.
2. Increased collaboration among teams within and among schools.
3. Increased understanding of the school improvement process.
4. Increased consistency in the implementation of reading and writing workshop.
5. Increased understanding of the New Illinois Learning Standards Incorporating the Common Core.

How did the staff initially respond to the Peer Coaching program, and how did their opinions, thoughts, and feelings change over time?

The initial reaction of our school teams to Peer Coaching varied from uncertainty and visible signs of discomfort to quick engagement in Peer Coaching. Two variables seemed to make the difference in our teams' initial reactions. Teams who had been meeting regularly to collaborate about improving student learning seemed to find Peer Coaching an easy next step for them. Peer Coaching seemed to give them a structure and process to follow. The second variable was principal leadership. If the principal had implemented team collaboration in previous years or if the principal is an active participant in professional development, assuming the role of learning beside his or her staff, those teams engaged in Peer Coaching more quickly. As the year of professional development continued, all the teams were observed to engage in increased collaborative conversations about improving teaching and learning, implementing reading and writing workshop, and implementing the New Illinois Learning Standards Incorporating the Common Core. Our schools are entering their second year of implementation and are gaining confidence in their use of Peer Coaching.

What do you see as the *benefits* and the *hurdles* of implementation?

Teacher willingness to enter into a coaching relationship with other teachers with whom they work on a regular basis is both a hurdle and benefit of Peer Coaching. It is a hurdle in terms of teachers initially being uncomfortable with letting other teachers witness them in the role of a learner. It is a benefit in terms of teachers becoming comfortable with the coaching process more quickly than other types of coaching because as the name implies, the participants are peers who bring expertise to the relationship. All types of coaching begin with establishing the coaching relationship, and resistance to the coaching process is a hurdle that must be overcome. The coaching relationship seems to develop more quickly with Peer Coaching because Peer Coaching recognizes that everyone has expertise and can learn from each other.

Were there any surprises along the way?

There were a couple of surprises along the way. The first surprise was the role of the principal in establishing the culture of coaching in the school. The principals of teams who adopted Peer Coaching more quickly demonstrated the following:

• They were actively involved in the professional development on Peer Coaching.

• They shared the role of leader during discussions with members of their team.

• They tended to ask questions such as "How could we…?" or "What do you think about…?"

• They encouraged teachers to share their ideas and be innovative.

Another surprise was that teams needed more practice time and more review of concepts than we initially planned. We found that if we did not incorporate enough practice time, teams seemed to regress between professional development sessions and had to regroup and review prior concepts. Teams who were meeting regularly to collaborate about teaching and learning seemed to experience less of this frustration.

When we increased the team time during the professional development sessions to practice or apply the concepts being learned, all the teams seemed to benefit.

Do you believe that the Peer Coaching effort benefited staff and student learning? How so?

Definitely yes. District 181 was in the process of implementing a new English language arts curriculum that aligned to the Common Core standards. The new curriculum also moved from using a basal reading program to a balanced literacy approach using reading and writing workshop. Because we had not yet developed our internal capacity for Peer Coaching, we used external coaches to support the first year of implementation. With the implementation of Peer Coaching, we have dramatically increased our capacity to support teachers in implementing new curriculum and instructional practices. In the near future, we will begin implementing new mathematics curriculum and instructional resources aligned with the Common Core standards. New science curriculum is also in the development stage. Peer Coaching will allow us to support teachers in the implementation of the new standards and curriculum when they need it and not just when the external coach can be scheduled.

In terms of student learning, parents and teachers are reporting improvement in student writing both in terms of quantity and quality. We began implementation of Common Core State Standards in mathematics in grade 3. We are seeing an increase in the percentage of 3rd grade students mastering 4th grade materials from 40 percent to 80 percent. Spring 2014 NWEA MAP results for 3rd grade students are promising, with a mean RIT of 217.2 and 73.6 percent meeting their individual growth targets (Note: 40–60 percent meeting individual growth targets is considered typical for schools, based upon NWEA norms).

What advice would you give to a team, school, or district considering a Peer Coaching program?

Based upon the research of Joyce and Showers and our experience in District 181, we would advise that coaching be part of any professional development plan in which the goal is consistent implementation with fidelity. We found that it is best to establish regular collaboration time and collaborative teams first, or if this is not feasible, at least concurrently. We recommend that school teams participate in Peer Coaching together and that the principal be an active participant. If your schools have building leadership teams, you may want to consider having this be the first team from each school to participate. We recommend beginning by establishing team norms and spending time on team development as you begin Peer Coaching. We also recommend incorporating team time into every training session so teams can practice coaching strategies or plan how they will share their new learning with their colleagues during an upcoming staff meeting.

What suggestions would you provide to ensure that a Peer Coaching program evolves over time to meet the changing needs of staff and students?

• Provide ongoing professional development on Peer Coaching—second-year sessions for the initial school team and an opportunity for new team members to participate in first-year training as a district cohort for developing coaches.

• Incorporate Peer Coaching into the job descriptions of key staff members such as reading specialists, gifted specialists, special education teachers, and media resource specialists.

• Incorporate Peer Coaching into building leadership and teacher collaboration time.

• Seek feedback from staff after each professional development session and at least annually regarding how to improve professional development, including Peer Coaching.

Any other insights you would like to offer as a result of your participation?

Peer Coaching takes time, and you will experience successes and challenges along the way. Expect midcourse adjustments, for this is the synergy that comes from the coaching process and is the origin of some of our best ideas. Finally, kindness, encouragement, and respect go a long way in fostering a culture of coaching.

Appendix B:
Sample Pre-Conference and Post-Conference Questions

℃ The Pre-Conference

The following questions are examples of what a coach might ask an inviting teacher during a pre-conference. These questions are not to be followed as a script, but rather are offered as samples. Most likely you would not ask every one of these questions. The coach's questions should be driven by the focus specified by the inviting teacher, as well as the inviting teacher's responses to the coach's previous questions. Coaching, like teaching, involves decision making.

Sample Questions

• What is the focus of the lesson? *OR* What will the lesson be about?

• What outcomes or standards will be addressed? *OR* What skills and knowledge will students develop?

• What will you do to open the lesson? Introduce concepts? Invite practice? Monitor student learning? Close the lesson? Invite reflection?

• What teaching strategies will you use to produce student outcomes? *OR* How will students be actively engaged?

• What student behaviors do you expect to see? *OR* What will students be doing as the lesson unfolds?

• What will students do that will let you know that they have mastered the lesson concepts? *OR* What student behaviors will indicate the lesson's success?

• What led up to the lesson? *OR* What learning experiences did students have in the lesson before this one?

• What would you like me to observe? *OR* How would you like me to focus the observation?

• Is it OK if I walk around and watch/speak to students during the observation, or would you prefer I stay seated and not interact? Where would you like me to position myself so that I am not interfering with the lesson?

• How would you like me to collect observational data (e.g., scripting, interaction analysis, questioning strategies, teacher behavior/student behavior notes, digital recording, other method)?

• Is there anything else you would like to share?

• Is there any other background information you would like me to know?

• Do you have any feedback for me about the questions I have asked? Are there any questions you wish I would have asked or would have asked differently?

The Post-Conference

The following questions are examples of what a coach might ask an inviting teacher during a post-conference. These questions are not to be followed as a script, but rather are offered as samples. Most likely you would not ask every one of these questions. A coach's questions should be driven by the focus specified by the inviting teacher during the pre-conference, as well as the inviting teacher's responses to the coach's previous questions. Coaching, like teaching, involves decision making.

Sample Questions

• As you reflect upon the lesson, how do you think or feel it went?

• Did students' behavior match your vision of success? What evidence of student learning did you notice?

• What do you recall about your teaching behavior? What did you do that generated the visible learning of students?

• As you ponder the outcomes or standards for this lesson, do you believe they were addressed? What did students do that informed your assessment?

• Were there places in the lesson where you changed your teaching strategy? What indicated that a change was needed?

• Did all students perform as you envisioned they would? If not, what's your hunch about why they did not or why they excelled?

• You asked me to look for _____. What do you recall about that?

• What learnings about teaching and student learning did this lesson generate?

• What will you do/ask students to do in the lesson that follows this one?

• Would you offer me feedback about the coaching strategies I used? What facilitated the way in which you reflected about and analyzed the lesson? Is there anything you wish I would have done differently?

Appendix C:
Topics for Peer Coaching Sessions

Note: These topics are examples that could be used during focused professional learning sessions about Peer Coaching. Each of these sessions is planned for a full day (5–6 hours).

Session 1: Overview of Peer Coaching

- What causes learning to occur?
- Exploring and analyzing factors that lead to high-quality teaching and learning: the goal of Peer Coaching
- Visible Learning and Peer Coaching
- Peer Coaching
  - A definition
  - Overview of the research on Peer Coaching
  - Building a coaching relationship
  - Trust and relationships among professional colleagues
  - A spectrum of collaborative work and formal coaching options (outside and inside the classroom)
  - Collaborative work structures (outside-the-classroom collaborative work); practice
- Planning for application with a colleague
- Reflections and personal next steps

Session 2: Formal Coaching

- Discussion of collaborative work experiences; problem solving
- Overview of formal coaching
  - Pre-conference (explanation of process, models, examples, practice generating and responding to questions)
  - Observation (overview of the process, practice)
  - Post-conference (explanation of the process, demonstration, practice generating and responding to questions)
  - Practice of the pre-conference, observation, and post-conference
  - Planning for application experiences with a colleague
- Reflections and personal next steps

Session 3: Observation Instruments

- Discussion of formal coaching experiences; problem solving
- Additional pre-conference and post-conference practice
- Feedback
- Overview of observation instruments
  - Scripting
  - Interaction analysis
  - Time off task
  - Verbal flow
  - Teacher made
  - Electronic options
- Planning for application with a colleague
- Reflections and personal next steps

Session 4: Factors Influencing Peer Coaching Relationships

- Discussion of practice tasks
- Overview of factors influencing Peer Coaching relationships
  - How we perceive the world
  - Core values

- Factors influencing thinking and behavior
  - Modality preferences
  - Learning styles
  - Personality styles
- Impact of preferences and styles on perception and language
- Planning for application with a colleague
- Reflections and personal next steps

Session 5: Fine-Tuning Communication Skills for Conferencing

- Discussion of application experiences
- Communication skills for conferencing (adapted from Costa & Garmston, 2002)
  - Presuppositions (explanation, modeling, and practice for each of these communication skills)
  - Clarifying
  - Paraphrasing
  - Reframing
  - Providing specific feedback
  - Using wait time
  - Neutral comments
  - Assertions of interest
  - Reciprocity
- Planning for application with a colleague
- Reflections and personal next steps

Session 6: Refining and Expanding Conferencing Skills

- Discussion of application experiences
- Advanced conferencing skills
  - Pre-conference
  - Observation
  - Post-conference
- Planning for application with a colleague
- Reflections and personal next steps

References

Armstrong, A. (2012, Summer). The art of feedback. *The learning system, 7*(4), 1–5.

Azzam, A. M. (2014, September). Motivated to learn: A conversation with Daniel Pink. *Educational Leadership, 72*(1), 12–17.

Barth, R. (1990). *Improving schools from within.* San Francisco: Jossey-Bass.

Berman, P. & McLaughlin, M. W. (1978). *Federal programs supporting educational change, vol. viii: Implementing and sustaining innovations.* Santa Monica, CA: RAND.

Bird, T., & Little, J. W. (1986). How schools organize the teaching occupation. *Elementary School Journal, 86*(4), 493–512.

Blase, J., & Blase, J. (2000). *Empowering teachers: What successful principals do* (2nd ed.). Thousand Oaks, CA: Corwin.

Bryk, A. S., & Schneider, B. (2004). *Trust in schools: A core resource for improvement.* New York: Russell Sage Foundation.

Carroll, T. (2009, October). The next generation of learning teams. *Phi Delta Kappan, 91*(2), 8–13.

Casey, K. (2006). *Literacy coaching: The essentials.* Portsmouth, NH: Heinemann.

Clutterbuck, D. (2005). *Creating a coaching climate.* Retrieved from http://pc4p.com.au/j14/images/stories/clutterbuck3.pdf

Costa, A. (2010). Cognitive coaching. Retrieved from http://education.jhu.edu/PD/newhorizons/strategies/topics/Cognitive%20Coaching/

Costa, A. L., & Garmston, R. J. (2002). *Cognitive coaching: A foundation for renaissance schools* (2nd ed.). Norwood, MA: Christopher-Gordon.

Danielson, C. (2012, November). Observing classroom practice. *Educational Leadership, 70*(3), 32–37.

Darling-Hammond, L. (2010). *The flat world in education.* New York: Teachers College Press.

Darling-Hammond, L. (2013, April 11). In V. Strauss, What teachers need and reformers ignore: Time to collaborate. *The Washington Post.* Retrieved from http://www.washingtonpost.com/blogs/answer-sheet/wp/2013/04/11/what-teachers-need-and-reformers-ignore-time-to-collaborate/

Deal, T., & Peterson, K. (2009). *Shaping school culture: Pitfalls, paradoxes, and promises.* San Francisco, CA: Jossey-Bass.

Dean, C. B., Hubbell, E. R., Pitler, H., & Stone, B. (2012). *Classroom instruction that works: Research-based strategies for increasing student achievement* (2nd ed.). Alexandria, VA: ASCD.

de Goeij, K. (2013). *Making meaning of trust in the organizational setting of a school* (Doctoral dissertation). University of Alberta, Canada.

Donaldson, G. A. (2008). *How leaders learn: Cultivating capacities for school improvement.* New York: Teacher's College Press.

Dozier, C. (2006). *Responsive literacy coaching: Tools for creating and sustaining purposeful change.* Portland, ME: Stenhouse.

Drago-Severson, E., & Blum-DeStefano, J. (2014, August). Change no to yes. *Journal of Staff Development, 35*(4), 26–29.

DuFour, R. (February, 2011). Work together: But only if you want to. *Phi Delta Kappan, 92*(5), 57–61.

Eaker, R., & Keating, J. (2008). A shift in school culture. *Journal of Staff Development, 29*(3), 14–17.

Fullan, M. (2002, May). Beyond instructional leadership. *Educational Leadership, 59*(8), 16–21.

Fullan, M. (2007). *The new meaning of organizational change* (2nd ed.). New York: Teachers College Press.

Fullan, M., Bennett, B., & Rolheiser-Bennett, C. (1989). *Linking classroom and school improvement.* Paper presented at the annual meeting of the American Educational Research Association, San Francisco.

Fullan, M., & Miles, M. (1992). Getting reform right: What works and what doesn't. *Phi Delta Kappan, 73*(10), 745–752.

Gallo, C. (2012, September 6). *7 sure-fire ways great leaders inspire people to follow them.* Retrieved from http://www.forbes.com/sites/carminegallo/2012/09/06/7-sure-fire-ways-great-leaders-inspire-people-to-follow-them/

Garmston, R. J. (1987, February). How administrators support peer coaching. *Educational Leadership, 44*(5), 18–26.

Garmston, R., Linder, C., & Whitaker, J. (1993, October). Reflections on cognitive coaching. *Educational Leadership, 51*(2), 57–61.

George, B. (2007). *True north: Discover your authentic leadership.* San Francisco: Jossey-Bass.

Glickman, C. (1990, September). Pushing school reform to a new edge: The seven ironies of school empowerment. *Phi Delta Kappan, 72*(1), 68–72.

Goldsmith, M., Lyons, L., & Freas, A. (2000). *Coaching for leadership: How the world's greatest coaches help leaders learn.* San Francisco: Jossey-Bass.

Goleman, D., Boyatzis, R., & McKee, A. (2002). *Primal leadership: Learning to lead with emotional intelligence.* Boston: Harvard Business School Press.

Guskey, T. (1995). *Results-oriented professional development: In search of an optimal mix of effective practices.* Retrieved from http://www.nrsweb.org/docs/trainings/summer2009/resultsorientedprofdev_guskey.doc

Hargreaves, A. (1989). *Teacher development and teachers' work: Issues of time and control.* Paper presented at the International Conference on Teacher Development, Toronto.

Hargreaves, A. (1994). *Changing teachers, changing times: Teachers' work and culture in the postmodern age.* New York: Teachers College Press.

Hargreaves, A., & Dawe, R. (1990). Paths of professional development: Contrived collegiality, collaborative culture, and the case of peer coaching. *Teaching and Teacher Education, 6*(3), 227–240. Great Britain: Pergamon Press.

Hargreaves, A., & Fullan, M. (2012). *Professional capital: Transforming teaching in every school.* New York: Teachers College Press.

Hattie, J. (2009). *Visible learning: A synthesis of over 800 meta-analyses relating to achievement.* New York: Routledge.

Hattie, J. (2012a). *Visible learning for teachers.* London and New York: Routledge.

Hattie, J. (2012b, September). Know thy impact. *Educational leadership, 70*(1), 18–23.

Hess, R., & Robbins, P. (2012). *The data toolkit: Ten tools for supporting school improvement.* Thousand Oaks, CA: Corwin.

Hirsch, S. (1995/1996, December/January). Approaches to improving schools start with developing a shared vision. *School Team Innovator.*

Hord, S., Rutherford, W., Huling-Austin, L., & Hall, G. (1987). *Taking charge of change.* Alexandria, VA: ASCD.

Joyce, B., & Showers, B. (1982). The coaching of teaching. *Educational Leadership, 40*(1), 4–10. Retrieved from http://web.ebscohost.com

Kantor, R. M. (1997). *On the frontiers of management.* Boston: Harvard Business School Press.

Kenney, J. M., Hancewicz, E., Heuer, L., Metsisto, D., & Tuttle, C. L. (2005). *Literacy strategies for improving mathematics instruction.* Alexandria, VA: ASCD.

Killion, J. (2009). Coaches' roles, responsibilities and reach. In J. Knight (Ed.), *Coaching: Approaches and perspectives* (pp. 7–28). Thousand Oaks, CA: Corwin Press.

Killion, J., & Harrison, C. (2006). *Taking the lead: New roles for teacher leaders and school-based coaches.* Oxford, OH: National Staff Development Council.

Kise, J. (2006). *Differentiated coaching: A framework for helping teachers change.* Thousand Oaks, CA: Corwin.

Knight, J. (2007). *Instructional coaching: A partnership approach to improving instruction.* Thousand Oaks, CA: Corwin.

Kruse, S. D., & Seashore-Louis, K. (2009). *Building strong school cultures: A guide to leading change.* Thousand Oaks, CA: Corwin.

Lerner, H. (2001). *The dance of connection: How to talk to someone when you're mad, hurt, scared, frustrated, insulted, betrayed, or desperate.* New York: Harper.

Lick, D. W., & Murphy, C. U. (Eds.). (2007). *The whole-faculty study group fieldbook: Lessons learned and best practices from classrooms, districts and schools.* Thousand Oaks, CA: Corwin.

Little, J. W. (1981). *School success and staff development: The role of staff development in urban desegregated schools—Executive summary.* Washington, DC: National Institute of Education.

Little, J. W. (1982). Norms of collegiality and experimentation: Workplace conditions of school success. *American Educational Research Journal, 19*(3), 325–340.

Little, J. W. (1985). Address to mentor teachers. Napa, CA.

Little, J. W. (1991). Presentation. Napa County Office of Education Mentoring Conference, Napa, CA.

Manthey, G., & Cash, J. (2014). Videre [software]. Lead Learner Associates.

Marzano, R. J. (2003). *What works in schools: Translating research into action.* Alexandria, VA: ASCD.

Miles, M., & Louis, K. (1987). Research on institutionalization: A reflective review. *Lasting School Improvement: Exploring the Process of Institutionalization.* Leuven, Belgium: OECD.

Nolan, M. (2007). *Mentor coaching and leadership in early care and education.* New York: Thomson Delmar Learning.

Parrett, W. H., & Budge, K. M. (2012). *Turning high-poverty schools into high-performing schools.* Alexandria, VA: ASCD.

Patterson, K., Grenny, J., McMillan, R., & Switzler, A. (2002). *Crucial conversations.* New York: McGraw-Hill.

Peterson, K. (n.d.). Is your school's culture toxic or positive? Retrieved from http://www.educationworld.com/a_admin/admin/admin275.shtml

Robbins, P. (1984). *The Napa-Vacaville follow-through research project* (final report). Washington, D C: National Institute of Education.

Robbins, P. (1991a). *The development of a collaborative workplace: A case study of Wells Junior High.* (Unpublished doctoral dissertation, University of California, Berkeley).

Robbins, P. (1991b). *How to plan and implement a peer coaching program.* Alexandria, VA: ASCD.

Robbins, P., & Alvy, H. (2014). *The principal's companion: Strategies to lead schools for student and teacher success* (4th ed.). Thousand Oaks, CA: Corwin.

Robbins, P., Gregory, G., & Herndon, L. (2000). *Thinking inside the block schedule: Strategies for teaching in extended periods of time.* Thousand Oaks, CA: Corwin.

Rosenholtz, S. (1989). *Teachers' workplace.* New York: Longman.

Saavedra, E. (1996). Teacher study groups: Contexts for transformative learning and action. *Theory into practice, 35*(4), 271–276. Retrieved from http://web.ebscohost.com/

Schlechty, P. C. (1993, Fall). On the frontier of school reform with trailblazers, pioneers, and settlers. *Journal of Staff Development, 14*(4), 46–51.

Schlechty, P. C. (2001). *Shaking up the schoolhouse: How to support and sustain educational innovation.* San Francisco: Jossey-Bass.

Schmoker, M. (2004). Tipping point: From reckless to reform to substantive instructional improvement. *Phi Delta Kappan, 85,* 424–432.

Schön, D. A. (1987). *Educating the reflective practitioner: Toward a new design for teaching and learning in the professions.* San Francisco: Jossey-Bass.

Scott, S., & McLain, B. (2011, April). Collaborative culture: Conflict is normal but learning to deal with conflict skillfully takes practice. *Journal of Staff Development, 32*(2).

Silver, S., & Hanson, J. R. (1996). *Learning styles and strategies.* Ho-Ho-Kus, NJ: Thoughtful Press.

Tomlinson, C. (2014). *The differentiated classroom: Responding to the needs of all learners.* Alexandria, VA: ASCD.

Tschannen-Moran, M. (2004). *Trust matters: Leadership for successful schools.* San Francisco, CA: Jossey-Bass.

Uebbing, S., & Ford, M. (2011). *The life cycle of leadership.* Oxford, OH: Learning Forward.

Wiggins, G. (2012, September). Seven keys to effective feedback. *Educational Leadership. 70*(1), 10–16. Alexandria, VA: ASCD.

Wiggins, G., & McTighe, J. (2005). *Understanding by Design* (2nd ed.). Alexandria, VA: ASCD.

Zepeda, S. (2012). *Professional development: What works* (2nd ed.). Larchmont, NY: Eye on Education.

Index

About the Author

Pam Robbins is an independent educational consultant who works with public and private schools, school districts, educational service centers, state departments of education, leadership academies, principal centers, professional organizations and associations, universities, and corporations throughout the United States and the world. Pam's professional interests include peer coaching, mentoring, brain research and effective teaching, instructional strategies for the block schedule, learning communities, leadership, supervision, the leadership practices of Abraham Lincoln, and presentation skills.

As an educator, Pam's experience includes serving as a special education teacher, intermediate-grades classroom teacher, high school basketball coach, and school leader. As an administrator, she served as Director of Special Projects and Research for the Napa (CA) County Office of Education and Director of Training for the North Bay California School Leadership Academy.

Pam earned her doctorate from the University of California, Berkeley. Her doctoral studies focused on teacher leadership and the development of learning communities. She was awarded the Best Dissertation Award by the National Staff Development Council.

Pam has authored or coauthored several articles, book chapters, and books. Publications include *How to Plan and Implement a Peer Coaching Program* (ASCD); *Thinking Inside the Block Schedule: Strategies for Teaching in Extended Periods of Time* (with Gayle Gregory and Lynne Herndon, Corwin); *If I Only Knew* (with Harvey Alvy, Corwin); *The New Principal's Fieldbook* (with Harvey Alvy, ASCD); *The Data Toolkit: Ten Tools for Supporting School Improvement* (with Robert Hess, Corwin); *A Professional Inquiry Kit on Emotional Intelligence* (with Jane Scott, ASCD); *The Principal's Companion* (with Harvey Alvy, Corwin); and *Learning From Lincoln: Leadership Practices for School Success* (with Harvey Alvy, ASCD). Pam may be reached at probbins@shentel.net.

Related ASCD Resources: Coaching and Collaboration

At the time of publication, the following ASCD resources were available (ASCD stock numbers appear in parentheses). For up-to-date information about ASCD resources, go to www.ascd.org.

Print Products

Engaging Teachers in Classroom Walkthroughs by Donald S. Kachur, Judith A. Stout, and Claudia L. Edwards (#113024)

How to Plan and Implement a Peer Coaching Program by Pam Robbins (#61191149)

Strengthening and Enriching Your Professional Learning Community: The Art of Learning Together by Geoffrey Caine and Renate N. Caine (#110085)

Creating Dynamic Schools Through Mentoring, Coaching, and Collaboration by Judy F. Carr, Nancy Herman, and Douglas E. Harris (#103021)

Building Teachers' Capacity for Success: A Collaborative Approach for Coaches and School Leaders by Pete Hall and Alisa Simeral (#109002)

Staffing the Principalship: Finding, Coaching, and Mentoring School Leaders by Suzette Lovely (#104010)

ASCD EDge Group

Exchange ideas and connect with other educators interested in differentiated instruction on the social networking site ASCD EDge™ at http://ascdedge.ascd.org/

The Whole Child Initiative helps schools and communities create learning environments that allow students to be healthy, safe, engaged, supported, and challenged. To learn more about other books and resources that relate to the whole child, visit www.wholechildeducation.org.

For more information: send e-mail to member@ascd.org; call 1-800-933-2723 or 703-578-9600, press 2; send a fax to 703-575-5400; or write to Information Services, ASCD, 1703 N. Beauregard St., Alexandria, VA 22311-1714 USA.